The Tin Prayer Words of the Wolverine

Notes From The Wild Testament

Steve Semken

Ice Cube Press
North Liberty, Iowa

The Tin Prayer:
Words of the Wolverine

second printing

The Ice Cube Press
205 N. Front Street
North Liberty, Iowa 52317
icecube@inav.net
www.icecubepress.com

Limited & Regional Edition
A Natural Prayer Publication

Manufactured in the United States of America

Printed on acid free, recycled paper
meeting library standards.

ISBN 1-888160-01-2

LCCN 00-104581

Printed and Bound by Publishers' Graphics, LLC

Supported in part with a grant from the Iowa Arts Council, a division of the Department of Cultural Affairs.

Thanks go out to Carolyn Servid and
Dorik Mechau of the Island Institute in
Sitka, Alaska for hosting me as writer-in-
residence during which I conceived of and
began the better part of what became
this essay.

I also received financial assistance from the
Iowa Arts Council for technical
as well as professional support. I would
be remiss if I didn't mention the boosts I
was given from Max dubah G-trout, Gary
Holthaus and Joan Liffring-Zug for their
efforts in helping me get to Alaska.
Thanks as well to Thomas Dean
and Richard Greene.
&
Whether in dreams, or real life I am
constantly getting inspiration, love and
well-beingness from Laura,
the cat house gang &
the glorious one just
become, Fenna Marie.

Choose one and pass it on:

"A flavor like brass in the sudden run of saliva in his mouth, a hard sharp constriction either in his brain or his stomach, he could not tell which and it didn't matter"
—William Faulkner

"I am invisible, understand, simply because people refuse to see me."
—Ralph Ellison

The glorious words of brave Bartleby,
"I would prefer not to."
—Herman Melville,

"The more we search for salvation and psychological cures the further away they become."
—Alan Watts

"The world as a work of art that gives birth to itself"
—Friedrich Nietzsche

Here I am, drifting on the teetering tottering point of imbalance. Right on the crux of the world's southern and northern hemispheres, am straddling the clock-way and counter-clock-a-way wondering about the drain swirl, about the second ticking swaddle, about that long dark drip down through vastness. I am wondering if you pull the plug then what, wondering which way my hair whirls.

Where I am there are mood swings rising and descending within fantasy, myth and dream. Which direction is truth going to go now? A lookinglass oughta woulda help. Spinning down, or up, left or right here in the straight sided center of the Wolverine's world, doubt rests in comfort. Here in the true center, smack dab in the middle you can forget about spinning. All you do is look out at the wheel of fortune twirling all roundabout in joy and sorrow, hot and cold, nice and mean, fiddle back to faddle.

In a confusing world of moral struggle what sounds so good is not so good deep down. You want to be a "true believer" right?, but who wouldn't want to be a true believer? Who wouldn't want to be considered fair and right? Think this though: If the shores of knowledge open us up to merely more contact with an infinite realm of mystery sea then is not headway in reverse knots? Is not the needle of penicillin causing disease thus built upon itself, is not the canned epoxy aerosol gaseous-ozone problem steeped from its own doing and getting worse and worse? Wouldn't a prayer have helped way back when, prior to the needle? Course if would've! You mess with the Wolverine then you're on your own sluggo, just don't come crying back to the roost saying your fancy ways wasn't the cause and that simple Shaman hope, Trinity ideologies and Astrological desires wouldn't or couldn't have helped. The narrow channel of reproducible fact differs wholeheartedly from clans who've observed good fortunes over long time.

Here's more. The laboratorium makes you feel ugly, sterile and god forsaken. The cathedral pits centuries of grace in your presence, a mound of badger dirt looms time eternal. Where do you want your truth coming from: gold leafed imagery, glory creamed stories & teethy grinned snakes, or inbred studied control groups which continue to sport their original, normalized, impersonal sin? On your death bed which will you turn to, what will you wish to hear, a song or a fact? Which one do you profess at the dinner table, at the grave side, when you start to sing, when you walk alone and observe the wind and the clouds and notice the tune of a creek bed flowing?

#2. For time beyond understanding I wandered in a daze, no matter what I looked at there was light leaking around the edges, was it confusion, or inspiration? The brightened, riza lacquered world seemed displayed through visions coated and imposing saturated gold

leaf. All interpretation lost, or was that all paradise found. Why can't the world be as an icon expressing the kingdom of all understanding without words? Think how it would save you right now. How blind we are then because we don't think visions can provide insight. Inside the cradle of pure light, exempt from shadows, are visible images, are halo's emitting the spirit of wide eyed life, deer blink clarity opening up. Try these beads:

Strip your stodgy crustaceous vicious blurry understanding
and get ye going forth to dreamy vision.
Gather close the toddy cozy of comfort friends,
where blurry glory people are all smiling, still, and known to be a resting.

#3. When's a Saint become a Saint, I'd bet at the moment of sublime aesthetic bliss, that moment when all truth is born, then shed, like the gushing karmic loss of a bodhisattva, resting calm as caterpillar in cocoon, otter in water, that epiphanic spurt of life when a word is a breath and sound is nothing more than wind, when all that's left is you on this side of hallelujah. This would give a need to celebrate mighty Saint Sudden. Born of an instant, an arresting handcuffing of epiphany. AND, if you're like me, anytime you're arrested the cause isn't evidently clear, and you're not all together willing. SO, there's Saint Sudden striking again.

Here are some more Saints. Saint Emo of Transcendence, clocks stopped in his presence, he swirled to life as though a drip-drop of southern hemisphere scorching down past the haunted realm of evil depths. What he thought became real, what he said was truth at all moments now and never. What people crave is this: the thick and juicy syrup of right-this-now-instant. Not Saint Emo, no he is understood only after rolling through slow motion. Lay person Fillmore Grin got Saint Emo on a winter day while laying heavy calm atop a heap of snowdrift, he'd went to thinking with the sun on his face and ski's at his feet about nothing 'cept the whole wide world above him and a dove it went to calling in his ears and there all-around him was a right-then brave new world. A world we've all at least once craved about.

The Wolverines, they're like Saint Ah-ha, a tricky Mechanic of Water, Fire, Earth and Air who seasons with pinches of oily Spirit. Saintly Seeden, she of virgin symbolic births, naughty dreams and blessed souls. A vowel messenger, uttering no more no less than "a e i o u," all together now and always all so so slowly aaaay-eee-iii-ohhh-yuuuu ...

There now, the drip of the celestial spheres has dropped and spread straight, not content with either counterclockwise, or correctwise. Just wet stillness straight down tight hollow confine into echo. Listen to the Wolverine, wild wilder wilderness, descending to a pin point at the center of prayer and time, released burdens, ending only as we look away look away o look away ....

pause
for magnificent revelations
when they appear
unexpectedly
as they will

Fearlessly quest
to find that place between
sunset and the ground
where the ferocious color green
straps the earth with
wrappings of sinuous root

Gut. Fish. Instinct. Fear. Cut. Hope. Moonshine. Gravy. I am a seed. I am the ground, I am that which has always been: realms of water, earth, fire and air. I am invisible and therefore I am.

Repetition makes up sense and this is how I start the day. Each morning I reach into the earth and pinch a small amount of always constant clay from the ground. Roll this pinch of earth between my fingers into a bead, place the bead of clay on my tongue then swallow, thus starting each morning with a dosage of wild rosary.

We come to know our place, our home, our hopes not by a mission, not by a career, not by a thought, but with the simplicity of bliss and faith. We must also literally eat and drink of where we reside. One should avoid taking where they live lightly. At the same time, one will do their place harm by trying too hard to know it. One will lose their soul, their religion by trying too much to have it. This is a world of backward principle. It must be observed while laughing and sneering.

When you get to know me it's no secret. I believe inspiration comes from only the simplest tasks. Once a week pick up trash in a public park. When you catch a ten inch brook trout feel blessed not immediately wishing for more. Everyday make sure you recycle. Be outdoors as much as possible. Discover hidden noises. Spot birds singing at water's edge. When you can, plant native seeds in the earth. Say what you really mean. Speak to those who need to hear you. It turns out that little acts are all we have to offer. Before you go to sleep thank something that made you smile that day, feel blessed with bouts of sadness. Read good poetry to friends and family at the dinner table. Enjoy your dreams. Live like it matters. Live outside yourself. Live deep within yourself. Envy the sound of crying, crave the songs of laughter. Live in bliss because you know who you are slowly becoming. Use candle light to gentle the dark on the way to sleep. Find faint visions hovering contentedly in corners.

... and so it goes like this. I offer you corn seeds, you offer me hospitality. I offer you my honesty, you offer me your trust. It doesn't take much imagination to understand what comes of all these things.

I offer no clear notion of the world. For the world offers itself always new. But I do believe that from a few simple things we forge faith, just as a tree branches with the sunlight and the soil and from seed. In fact, these types of things are what make the sun rise. Are the mysteries we must sleep shut-eyed easy with.

Then there is speed. Speed is overrated and a definite lie. I've wallowed a long time on the nectar of lies. Only a hummingbird is born to move at such full speed. As a result it has been years since I last stooped to pray.

When I knelt down I was uncertain which direction my mind would move. Would my prayer take me to the realm of blue Jupiter, or would it flap as shardy mirrored foil in the breeze. I was aware that faith and hope had eluded me for so long that the best I could do was search for a color. This search was not a game though. I knew that this color would mean everything to me. I believed the color I was in search of was an invisible ghost, perhaps prairie gold lined up in rows, or maybe the fleeting image of a pebbled trout shadow over water lacquered stones. I wasn't sure what would become of my prayer, but I had decided this was the smallest of matters. I reveled in that timeless thought we have all heard somewhere before, "Whatever will be will be." I was ready to live with the slowly comfortable, continual balm of mystery.

Years and years ago this had almost worked. I vaguely remember feeling the color I wanted. During a dream three Wolverines emerged from the forest. They were smelling the earth, gathering food when we spotted each other. They so naturally appeared I quickly became bewildered, shy and scared. A moment passed while we examined each other. My nerves clumped and dropped down my stomach with the clapping bind of thunder, forming a ball of winding doubt and fear at once, although I knew not to run, not to jolt away in fear I did so for ten quick strides then looked behind me with unexpected terror, posing the calmness of a whirlpool. Beyond my expectations these creatures instead of charging offered to let me join them, waving me to follow. This was my invitation to bliss, to experience the variety of existence amongst rich and wild reality. It was as if geese were barking soaring roaring in my ears. A spark of astonishment gushed through me. Yet, I couldn't, wouldn't believe that these spirits, these animals, were asking me to merge into the folds of the wild with them. *Who cared that I wanted this? What difference did it make I had waited for such an invitation?* I had hoped that someday I could exit the life we all know as human and instead be one with the wild world, grasping always wide-open spontaneity, becoming part of places void of time, existent in the soothing blanket of reliable instinct where passions become tied with survival. I had wanted to rid myself of worrisome hollow sleep disorders. To dash into a place deeper than dichotomy; off away from where always rusing rights and wrongs control the brain, off away from such simple and narrow minded sayings as good and evil. I had hoped to escape sitting and listening to instructions, the continual wishing within the eventual frustration of currency and its inherent dependency and poverty. I glared at the Wolverines, gawked like a hawk, ticked my head and eyes like a chicken. But a stunted grunt of full blooded doubt cracked and needled then popped aboundingly throughout me. Indecision strangled and seeped into the air, into my blood, into my mind and off of my tongue.

Curses and lockjaw!?! Why won't the mind work when most needed, why does thought so quickly confound and interfere? As generosity waved my way what I did is unexplainable. When offered a chance to join with my dreams I had suddenly stuttered, clutched and declined. There I stood then, having refused to merge with the Wolverines. Where the butterflies and doubts fluttering in my throat came from, how they overtook my rib cage and tongue I wasn't sure. What good is a hope if no faith be placed in it?

I had thought *No* and right then, just like greasy blowing tips of grass in steady windy motion, it was at once of an instant too late to change. The Wolverines peered mournfully at me and did what they needed to do, had to do, must do—disappeared. My primal gutted instinct and desires are what they wanted not my nary second thoughts.

So, I wasn't ready. No one to blame but myself. All the same, there went my dream—vanished before me into the deepening evening green of forest. All I could do was wonder. What had I done? How would I get the Wolverines to come back? For I had already changed my mind, *"Let me join you! Come back!"* I declared with sheer urgency, but to an empty forest now. I stared into the green of the forest and wondered what I'd done. The silence was deafening, the sun seemed to brighten and I remember taking a moment to admire the greening drops of light around me.

And here my friends was destiny before me: Was I to go forth in denial, with hope, or rather with regret? Would I choose to hope and find, or sit and tear and emit bemoans for chances shackled, lost and left behind.

Would I think of life as easy and out of grasp, or as continually needing hope and mission?

A decade passed. Then another five years without any hint of prayer. Why try. That is, until my above-mentioned kneeling in search of a vaguely felt color deep within. I had remained so ashamed at my failure to accept wishes and dreams that I had lived paralyzed with a brash and sarcastic, sharpened fork three tongued heart; perhaps taking the all-too-famous road less traveled, but also wandering down that even less known trail, that road that splits off of even the road less traveled. I had entered a spot in which I wanted no more than to fact find faults and failure. I started to think I hated others, when in fact I really hated myself. I slowly came to understand that hate of another was just a personal demise. An indication of how I couldn't accept all of myself, or all of what has been created. Similar to how humans now often treat the earth, without respect.

I seemed determined to think stories were no good to me and I suppose they weren't if I wouldn't enter, hear and believe in them. This fifteen years was mostly silent then, a time of going through the motions, itches not itching, and if itching not scratching, and if scratching then not where it itched.

What really happened is that I wasn't ready to believe in dreams. No one jumps so easily aboard their personal journey, goes through this micro-quick-flash of life without treading water and obtaining the sense of drowning. If you haven't overcome fear, haven't questioned and gone off alone from what has been expected of you, then I truly doubt that you have started your journey. Whosoever says that personal faith and imagination and dreams come easy know something other than dreams and imagination and faith. Nothing prepares you for their anchoring force and saturating comfort. In the front of your mind they are play toys, the silly methods of children—all talking wild hyperbole in chatty echo fashion. In the back of your brain they are churning with life. Given enough courage, if you try hard enough, imitate enough rivers in your thought and walk will you be able to capture wishes and act upon dreams. Only then can you become festively dependent on creativity, reliant on imagination. Although I have yet to rediscover the Wolverines I know they are out there, walking, growling, hunting, moving with all the elements of creation. Sometime we will cross paths again and at that moment I will be ready to shut my mouth and get in line with them. I will be able to dissolve and disappear, ebbing into the misty rich humus realm of deep dreams, that murky place where all things become as one. Where spirit is as real as dream and where bone is inside out of marrow.

This is the hard part of course. The waiting, the keeping of the faith. Just because you wish for revelation to come to you doesn't mean it will arrive the next instant. It's the opposite you see, you need to wipe clear your slate of mind games. Need to be willing to reach out and hug mystery for no reason, expecting absolutely nothing in return. This is nothing new though, living without fear and desire. This is what the Buddha has professed for eternity.

It turns out that there are no shortcuts and a definite lack of clear reason in all of this which is contrary to life as we think we want to know it. To declare confidence in the path of myth and imagination is becoming harder and harder in our day and age for many reasons. One reason is because of the ever-growing tribe of self-assured fact finders in our midst. Does truth require such convincing I wonder? Such formulas? Such money funding and herdings of speciality and all with such speed and urgency. I, for one, am not anxious for the new answers to life because they seem separate from hope and dreams. Is not standing in a natural shrine admiring a glen, a fen, a stream, a sunset enough to live off of, enough to know? There are stacks of literature by desert mystics, of wanderers, who understand life just fine without technology and in fact pass on deep and valuable knowledge. Why not stop and pause the body and mind and spirit in the beauty of blue Jupiter light? Is not the length of commitment to traditional myths and dreams a comforting enough depth to convince us that we don't have to know anything for certain.

Truth once uttered though, proceeds with swift assurance. Declared correctly it requires no more than the nod of the head while the brain revs up approval. It settles like good flavors, instantly and securely. The mouth can't help itself with the sudden blurt of a quickened and unhesitating, "Ah-ha!" Are not small relics constantly being left behind in honor of Saint Sudden. I ask you, who needs replication and peer review? Who needs them except perhaps the pathological marketing, money dependent soldiers of socially serious, career enabling knowledge hunters. I don't get it, what would be so great about understanding the world anyway?

Specialists insist on progress of a measurable sort. Faster computers, quicker access times, levels of verisimilitude and virtuality. All is based on such speed, on bell curve statistics and all with the assertion and expectation that the "correct way" is out there somewhere, we just haven't found it yet, but with hard work and proper funding the *truth* will be discovered, maybe in a distant galaxy, or deep in some hidden microscopic pattern within strands of DNA? Many believe that once all things have been explored, and only then, can we relax in a secure vision of truth, but the world is beyond any form of measurement, beyond finally knowing, well beyond anything as petty as some ultimate truth and will always be this way. Even if someone did declare to know something it would still only be the beginning. Unfortunately most people expect the truth, are relying on the truth to solve any and all problems that may occur.

I always say life is too short to go fast. Instead take comfort that your dreams are another's dreams, that myths are myths all over the world. I read recently a Shaker statement that went as follows: "Do all your work as though you had a thousand years to live, and as you would if you knew you must die tomorrow." I couldn't agree more. I also believe that you should feel satisfied that your deep thoughts and assumptions about reality are essentially just like anothers. Similarity is all around just because it is. Doesn't this eliminate the need for speed, of questing for truth? It's not just a coincidence that similarities abound. In many ways truth is constant at each and every moment yet varies from spot to spot and moment to moment. There are as many ways to see a tree as there are spots and ways to look at one. Yet this variety is remarkably common.

Witness the work of Joseph Campbell and his book entitled The Hero With A Thousand Faces. This is an entire life study realizing that we need to trust symbols and make sense of our deep assumptions and creativity, as Freud said, "The truths contained in religious doctrine are after all so distorted and systematically disguised that the mass of humanity cannot recognize them as truth."

Nothing can proceed as quickly as the current computer craze without a backfire, and I don't really mean with the equipment so much as in the head. The highest virtual computer environment is nowhere near the virtuality of a dream, or simply walking down the street for that matter. Dreams are constructs from the deep realm of unconsciousness, where faith and reality and truth and story reside. An interactive web page may be a step along the staircase of simple rational constructs, but infinite rods and visions from reality and dreams.

I know that when I got my first computer I was all excited about how it was going to suddenly make me a great and fluid, lavish and precise writer. I anxiously raced through the installation. Got everything turned on and double clicked to activate my fancy word processor that contained all the technical skills I had previously lacked, and which would allow my brain to open up to whole new wonderlands of conception. As I opened a new file I discovered the hoax. There I was, the computer humming along, but faced with what I had been faced with so many times before, empty space. It wasn't long before I was checking to see if my new computer had some games on it. Of course my unconscious was teaching me a lesson, confirming that my imagination and creative powers were still under my control and direction. One must be kidding when they declare that computers are essential to be alive in the 21st century. Sure they're nice and all around us, but *essential*, absolutely not!

A brief glimpse into our false dependency on scientific creation and literal fact based certainty was the recent Y2K rollover. This was a problem with our categorizing existence and time via a clock. This whole time thing is not real, although it does make very good sense in certain narrow, social situations. There are many ways to mark the continuation of life. We just happen to prefer living according to the Gregorian calendar and an agreed upon span of sixty second minutes. Really though, unless you were fascinated with Armageddon, there was never any question that the sun would rise on Jan. 1, 2000, the fear was that life as many of us wanted it to be might not join the sun. What a terrible place to have been if you were computer dependent. It was the world of the schizophrenic. No wonder the New Year's parties were so wild and tense, they were entirely inspired by fear!

If we get tricked into living a virtual life, into substituting e-mail contacts with face to face encounters, if we confuse web pages with actual experiences then we have committed what is often considered by many the most unforgivable sin of all: not paying attention and of leading an unresponsive life.

Do I really think we will lose creativity? No. It is part of everything we do, in fact, it is all any of us really do. Thinking we can repress and control creativity is only possible with words, it is like saying you can hold a heaping handful of water, or sand. It may sound possible, but try it.

I am uncomfortable with opinions whether from science, or religion that tell us how to use our creativity. That if we don't look at an Orthodox icon and see what "they" want us to see then we have abused the icon in some way, that we aren't in the know. This isn't how art, or anything, works, The world's not what any of us think it is, not what any of us want it to be, it just is, right now. Or as my wife is rumored to have said in her childhood.

"Laura, why's this bread taste good?"

The insightful response: "Because it is good!"

It's pretty simple really. You'll go crazy thinking about thinking. Try letting hopes and trust equal reality.

There is no way to control creativity consciously, yet it is limited unconsciously and that's good enough. We are biologically destined to create, are creations, are alive because of creation. Each night we lay down and the potential for dreams takes over us. Or we decide to drink a glass of water while reading, that's a creation. We put on a certain shirt, that's creation. We take a certain path in a forest, that's creation. That we created computers is not a problem. The problem is that fiction and creativity are taken so lightly and pushed aside as though a thing we do in infancy. People hear what they want to hear, but many hear things in a serious, career oriented, repressed way all the time and are so greedy and so competitive and so pompous and uncaring that they forget about joy. They hear a passage such as this, "When I was a child, I spake as a child, I understood as a child, I thought as a child: but when I became a man, I put away childish things." (1Corinthians 13:11) and think that kid stuff should be forsaken. Now to me this is a beautiful passage, but not if taken the wrong way, not when you give up the core of childish things. If you combine them with your new adult skills then you'll be able to put a herd of monkeys in your head and still get to work on time while travelling through the lost land of the Byzantine empire, or crossing Hadrian's wall in just the nick of time to answer a customers question. Yet how many people do all of us know who declare either verbally, or with their constantly slumped shoulders, "I shall be serious and never laugh again in my life." How many have left behind what they used, learned and laughed with? How many have lost and no longer utilize their "childish ways."

Why this is, is beyond me. Perhaps society has implanted a majority of people with the idea that society is in control of people and that individuality, childish hopes and such are to be banished for the good of all. This way of thinking certainly helps the minority of people who employ the majority of people so they can then take vacations to the Bahamas and drive around their commuter towns in highly expensive cars, laughing all the way to the bank. Being somber, serious and willing to frown is certainly considered the truth by the majority of people who call themselves adults for some odd reason. Those who have given up on childish inspirations, hopes and dreams and expect to be numb and sad the rest of their lives.

You surely know those people who are unable to retire, unable to feel alive without a job title. In Henry Melville's story, Bartleby, the tyranny of the majority won't stand for anyone running around with personal preferences. Won't stand for any interference with business and thus insist on the oppression of individuality. The saddest thing I know of is someone who has no life without their career, their job. Perhaps they retire and they can think of nothing else to do but go back to work, or slouch into an easy chair and in a twist of fate essentially become what they always feared and hated the most during their lives: unemployed. Just think of it, to have lived without ever devising a way to live on your own, to have discovered nothing that fills your heart with such passion that you can't help but be taken away into a netherworld of activity and contemplation to spots and ways of thought you've never encountered before. One might say they are inspired by their job, I suppose that works. Perhaps though they just can't change, just haven't thought of anything else to do, are too scared to change. Who knows?

Individuality is slightly feared of course. The usual response being that if everyone just went around doing what they wanted then there'd be a bunch of brightly colored, scantly dressed love bent killers on the loose high on drugs. Being fearful of individuals going amuck when immersed in creativity and individuality is completely unfounded and irrational though. As stated, humans are bound by their myths and own natures. It makes no sense to be mostly a killing creature, it makes no sense to be in favor of chaos. Children and their wild imaginations are treated as funny and trite by many adults and even most adolescents. Watch the face of a tenured scientist when a child declares that dragons taste like rainbows, or that red leaves falling on the ground are the footprints of a faraway and powerful Sun Spirit named Alvin. Heck even watch the face of a Priest with these types of comments. The very idea of it, that a free spirited individual with a new and seemingly ludicrous idea might be able to roam the earth and have an influence on human truth is considered dangerous even though all thoughts are entirely limited by being human.

I am stunned by the number of people who don't think they dream and simply don't care. Surprised by the number of people who can't sleep at night and declare this with no consideration of doing anything about it. Almost seem proud of the not sleeping, at least seem proud of complaining about it and thus lack the chance to dream. What a drought, what a sad repression, what fears these people must be harboring, what confusion! What uncompleted individualized lives.

Majorities prefer to establish facts (you can also call them laws) and want minds to stay within these laws. This allows, "right ways," to be measured and to have stamps of approval appropriately doled out. In this way of thinking, repression plays a big part of fact in my eyes. Rationality, "rightness", laws! Philosopher Ludwig Feuerbach once wrote, "Man cannot get beyond his true nature. He may indeed by means of the imagination conceive individuals of another so-called higher kind, but he can never get loose from his species." So once again I wonder, what's the worry everyone?

Fear not creation and imagination all ye gentle men and women. Whether we create Gods in our image, or vice versa, isn't really the point. Since all is creation, all is interpretation and therefore subject to always twisting, continual and everchanging interpretation. In addition, we aren't intended to really know God anyway. God is a deep deep deep concept, beyond knowing, way down past the realm of assumptions and moral conduct. Possessing some sort of final understanding will never happen, ever! Anyone who thinks differently didn't hear the songbird singing today, didn't hear the roots of prairie grass growing yesterday. Didn't see the sun set, or notice the water dripping just now. Thinking we can fully understand is a dangerous desire full of self-centered wishes for perfection.

Our myths and stories are who we really are and evidence of our most believable efforts as a species. Our stories and our myths are our real origins and our evolution. They are examinations of wish and hope, loss and love, our pathways through journey. The more you get involved in something, the more you think you know, yet the less you do and thus the further away the end becomes. As a result each of us had better hope the journey we call life is good enough. We best believe that we can die without knowing anything. If a person can't come to terms with needing merely trust and faith, love and laughter, at all times mixed with a devilish grin, then they will have lived without passion, without making peace with being alive in my opinion.

This is why I am so enamored by an old saying that goes, "What's more true than the truth? Well, the story of course." Or as Señor Jorge Luis Borges says, "My story will be true to reality or, in any case, to my personal memory of reality, which amounts to the same thing."

2.

There are no truths in the world of humans. We merely trick ourselves with beginnings. Each new idea in life is a good and honest start, which to a certain extent ends immediately. Ernest Hemingway roughly stated in one of his works, a writer should proceed with as much honesty as possible, stating each word slowly and truthfully. This holds as noble and decent advice. For it's true, good writing, as good living, is no more than collecting good and honest words, as well as pathetic mistakes, together with real efforts. From time to time you hope to reach a version of reality which your mind can rest with for a while. As for reaching the truth, or worse yet, some version of perfection, don't even fool yourself. The Gods of laughing will merely giggle unendingly in your face, and rightly so, any embarrassment suffered upon any declaration of perfection will be well deserved.

When I was growing up and going through college all I ever heard was that we needed scientists, and mathematicians in addition to smart business majors so that our nation could become strong. If we all picked these majors somehow we would better able to defend ourselves against the brutal and evil world being led by the so-called Communists, headquartered in the Soviet Union. A land and place which was slowly getting stronger and stronger and which apparently had very limited goals—that of overtaking the United States, and then to steal our countries math formulas and poorly protected money. As college kids we owed it to society, to our parents for pete's sake, to help make our country stronger by learning math and science as best we could. In many ways it felt like you weren't a wholehearted, red white and blue blooded citizen of the United States if you weren't majoring in some form of science, engineering, or business.

I don't remember hearing a national call for stories, poets, or myths. It didn't, and still doesn't seem to cross anyone's mind that stories are the best tools we have to understand the world and ourselves. How cool would it be if a Presidential candidate were going around telling the nation ancient myths, native and regional stories in their bid for President. How much more sense it would make if our State Senators would plead for fiction, plead for dreams and epiphanies, revelations and a real appreciation for where we each live. Stories strengthen the world, are prayers to mystery and hope. At once they are individual and public. Just think how real writers such as Gabriella Garcia Marquez, Jorge Luis Borges, Octavio Paz, Pablo Neruda have made their South American world. These writers have done more than math could ever do, these writers have created a truly rich and vivid world, stronger than a world convinced of its superiority because it cherishes the vagueness of two, or three, four, or five ... .

My first chance at becoming captivated by imagination and myths was confusing though, maybe it is for everyone. As a small boy with my tattered haircut and roaming knees I refused to believe in miracles. My parents didn't encourage or believe in miracles as far as I could tell, but when I was old enough to comprehend conversation my grandmother sat me down and explained how the world was created in six days, followed with a day of rest, by an elderly man with long white hair she said was named God. This came as a big surprise to me.

Then she went on to tell me about an ark and a rainstorm that lasted forty days and forty nights. I sat bewildered. She also hinted that this man she called God was overseeing everything in the world and that I needed to behave well or else bad things would happen to me. Where were these ideas coming from? My grandmother didn't seem capable of such fantastic stories. Was it possible for one person to oversee the world, the universe? I didn't know whether to believe her or not.

Later that day I told my brother about these unusual stories. He thought they seemed possible, but I admitted to him that I didn't think they could be. I asked him not to tell my grandmother though, but of course he did. We sat in her car, just about to drive to town, when he revealed my secret doubt. She immediately turned around and stated, "Why, Steven, any Grandson of mine WILL believe in God." Buckled down in the backseat of the car I nodded that yes, yes I did believe in God. This is where my mind stopped though. I didn't think about, or contemplate the existence of what I considered to be miracles, or some grand overseer of life such as God again until many years later.

Strangely enough though I did believe in made up characters wholeheartedly while growing up. This isn't much different than a miracle really, I just didn't know it. I guess I've always had a tendency toward fiction and imagination to explain the world. I invented a heroic friend/man named Coig who traveled and played with me for about a year and a half. I would have wild adventures with this character of mine on the staircase of our house, in our kitchen cabinets, next to the creek in our back yard. Coig survived every adventure I put him though. The only thing he didn't survive was my mind. At about five years old I began to make the slow, but required transition from imagination and creativity toward work and reality, toward group-mindthink games and sensibilities. I began to play football and follow all the rules of the game. I started making forts and dams in the woods with my neighbors and we all tried hard to get along. Rules started to become part of everyday life.

Still a lot of this was fantasy. I believed me and my friends were the best football players in the entire world. I was certain that we were the only ones that knew the mysterious ways of making stick and bark forts. I remember being puzzled when I started kindergarten that I was no longer the strongest man alive the way I had been in my adventures with Coig. I got into a scuffle with another kid and found out that I couldn't just will him to fall on the ground. He was as strong as I was, which was extremely disappointing to me. The world I had been living in was not entirely real in some way. It turned out that life would involve some adjusting to.

I didn't give up easily though. During show-and-tell in Kindergarten I would relate stories that I made up on the spot while our class sat in a big circle on the floor. I remember great events happening in this circle. For instance I discovered time. As though by magic it was revealed to me that the year was 1969. The way I was told this must have seemed fascinating because I've always remembered this revelation and how I came to understand that the world was progressing in some way and that I was part of it.

I also went on to disclose my own wild ideas from this circle. When show-and-tell finally did come around I would create. Although I had never seen a bear in the wild before, I claimed that once when my family was camping a giant black bear broke into our tent and ate all our food and sent my mom screaming to the car. I stated that the bear was really quite nice and even smelled good. I made up another wild story about an ostrich that buried its head in the yard when our dog started barking at it. I had stories of anteaters that lived in our house, of monkeys that made me sandwiches to eat in the woods, of roosters that played hide-and-seek. I was never sure at the time if the teacher knew I was making things up or not though. She never stopped me from sharing my stories. As far as I could tell the other kids seemed convinced too. To this day I can't tell you if I thought I was telling the truth or not, I think I believed what I said and that it was just a matter of time before all these things really did happen to me, or perhaps, and this is probably the real truth, I believed that what you thought was as good as what you really did, especially since I had been getting along just fine as a citizen in the realm of stories and dreams for a few years already.

This story telling didn't even last through the first grade though. For one thing, we no longer had a show-and-tell period, just work assignments and prolonged periods of time during which we listened to the teacher tell us what to think and do and read. This whole method of learning and of being judged according to what you could memorize and recite back to the teacher began another round of miracle stunting for me. It turned out that there was no way to mess around with the math problems I was being asked to solve, it turned out that these seemingly nice women who were my teachers wouldn't let me do whatever I wanted. I was slow to understand that drawing and telling stories was not part of the reward system. That leaving your seat and walking around was not even allowed. My teachers had created a full set of rules which all of us had to follow, or else we would get in trouble. I often thought that surely the rules weren't real, or didn't apply to me for some reason.

Whenever I got in trouble in those early years I vaguely remembered my Grandmother's warning that God was watching everyone and punishing the bad. I wondered if perhaps I better behave correctly, or worse yet, maybe it was already too late. When I did get in trouble though it didn't seem to me like I had really done anything wrong. Then I wondered who was actually right, the teacher or me. Who would my Grandmother's God side with? The hoax, which I doubt that I understood at the time, was that eventually I did follow the rules, but not honestly. I was just pretending to be good according to the rules and not get in trouble. I never believed much of what was supposed to be good was really all that good. Really most of it wasn't, the rules were just devised as a sort of day care system to manage the human resources in the schools.

Not knowing, or ever being told any more about religion than the fact that God created the world and punished those who did wrong, I probably started getting worried and extremely confused regarding stories and expected behavior though.

It quickly became clear to me by the middle of first grade that everyone in my class was expected to learn and behave exactly the same and in addition to learning we needed to behave quietly! Being different was not something that would have been tolerated, making up stories would have been against the rules, perhaps even punishable by a mild form of force. I'll never forget Neal Price being dragged and yanked, glasses in his right hand, across the top of his desk, into the "teacher's room" for making a funny noise and goofy face while the teacher was talking. We all made sure there were no teachers around before we goofed off after that.

I stand before you now and declare I've returned to stories though and so-called make-believe. I tried to be a physics major. I excelled at math much against my wishes (apparently calculus comes naturally to me). I have plundered the world of sales and money, studied the history of the world, worn suits and ties, focused intently on the reality of customer service and believe they all lack life.

It seems fairly obvious that society prefers to manhandle individuals for the good of a few: whether it's Corporate Presidents, Leaders of Pathological and Fundamentalists churches, or just a night manager in a restaurant, once given power most use it to abuse and take a fast track to self-importance. Imagination (which is essentially synonymous with individual) is the only vital source of knowledge I feel comfortable with. It can slay dragons, create mountains and produce virgin births. It turns out, through the study of myth, that it is what we create with our imagination that our species can all agree upon.

Believing in myths seems to have lots of downfalls though. For instance you end up not really knowing anything in a proper manner and have other adults constantly pointing out to you that you're wrong; that you're living in a fantasy world. You'll probably have to remind yourself that it's okay not to make much money since myths aren't big business these days. In a lot of ways you're forced to live with multiple personalities. A fake one you use on the public and a real one you live with and are committed to.

If we use our imagination we can climb to the clouds on a bean pole. Living with story is outrageously vital. As I mentioned, humans can't imagine beyond themselves, we just can't. And not only that, we get our thoughts for nothing, they just happen inside us. Repression filters and controls them over time if you let them.

I would say that the real world IS that of gathering wild berries, carrying water, canning tomatoes, laughing at our children, sawing wood, humming songs, hunting deer, carrying on conversation with our friends, having a wild imagination and believing what seems real. To think more of ourselves is pure greed and pits us once again in front of life's temptations: desire and fear. Why not try to live fluidly, contentedly amongst suffering, accepting what IS instead always striving so concretely for what we have been convinced by the economy that we are supposed to want.

Like I said, story telling is bounded by our being human, this doesn't mean we are in any way limited, or not living alongside mystery. Doesn't mean we aren't exploring the world around us. We will not use up the world through dream or imagination. We can frolic all over the place, think thoughts to their extremes without danger. As stated by Lao Tzu in the Way of Life:

"when you know
what is eternally so,
you have stature ...
and when divinity is the Way
Which is final
Then, though you die,
You shall not perish."
(v.16)

3.

The unconscious force of life in the Midwest floats inside the air rather than in the sea. A tornado is a whale moving through pouring rain. Hot and humid air from the Gulf of Mexico, forced to try and coexist beside cold, dry air from the Arctic never seems to work. They are totally unable to get along with a friendly handshake, instead they smash and scatter and lurch across open space, treating the whole of the open prairie as a landing pad.

When a big storm comes rumbling along in the sky during a summer day it's normal to spot people peering and eeking out their windows. Crowds gather near breakroom doors, everyone pondering, respecting, acknowledging the noises and flashes of lightning above. You'll see scores of folks suddenly sitting on their front porches, other people will pop open their lawn chairs, raise their garage doors and stare at the world above with hope and bewilderment as if their dreams were coming to life.

While everyone's looking up, and if the wind gets to kicking enough, eyes will start looking out into the horizon even further. If the air becomes greenish and gelatin-like everyone will sit still and wonder what to do. *What if a tornado comes barreling through?* It's like a whale spewing toward the surface of sea water, rising, rolling, descending with a broad and mighty tail, teasing our minds with deep dark thoughts. With every flash of lightning comes possibility, wisdom, the stones which build our hopes toward faith. The mind of the storm watcher twists and wonders, thoughts mend with strands of falling rain as though Captain Ahab searching the wide open seas for his living obsessive, nightmare.

During these Iowa storms the emergency sirens almost always go off since living alongside the natural world is something most people have been convinced they need to fear and be warned of, as though the weather were like enemy bombs being dropped. These sirens are supposed to warn everyone that a disaster is on the way, yet as far as I know they are always wrong, going off because lightning strikes a fuse box or something. Not many that I know of take these sirens seriously, yet the sirens do seem to give anchor to fears, justifying the thoughts of dread that so many people briefly let run through their brains as storms arrive and open up full throttle. I just consider the sirens a type of alarm clock stating that dreamtime has arrived.

I remember when they first installed the siren system. I was in first grade and at that time I was thankful such a system had been put in place since

I was most definitely scared of tornadoes. I just hoped I would be able to hear the blaring screeches of the siren system when I needed to. One weekend afternoon during a thunderstorm the wails of the emergency siren went off. At that point I was truly terrified. I made sure my brother followed me under the stairs. This was no small venture as normally I was frightened of the stuff and the space under the stairs, so many strange boxes and items rested way back in there and where the end of the space went, down into the ground with ghosts, I didn't know. With the sirens blaring I ignored the silent bulking suitcases and boxes though, dashing for what I'd been told was the safest place in our house. Once we were stowed away beneath the stairs we wondered what would happen next. *How long do we wait? Would a police car drive by and announce it was safe to come out?* My mom had gone under the stairs with us and we all sat there not knowing what to do, waiting for our next direction.

After we could no longer hear the sirens, or the wind, or the rain we peaked out the door of the stairwell, through one of the back windows of the house and could see the sun was shining. We left our confines, figuring it was safe. Later we learned that the sirens had gone off by mistake, lightning had hit one of the switches.

I had ventured into fear for no reason. I was appalled. What good was fear if it wasn't real. Too bad the Buddha hadn't been nearby right then, he would have patted me on the shoulder. Keep that thought he would have stated. Now let's work on ridding you of desire.

I still remain awed by thunderstorms, marvel at their wildness, but the sirens don't mean much to me anymore. I am amused, as well as frustrated, at the increased chaos these sirens contribute. In the heart of the worst storm everything goes berserk. I mean all the dogs begin to wail and bark in concert with the thunder and wind and sirens. Streaks of lightning trails scatter as if the veins inside the great and giant brain of some magnificent Wizard from the often times mocked realm of Oz. All of life is swept up and jostled across the pan of the sky. It seems as though there's always a freight train blasting through during a storm as well. The train's whistle growling past each street intersection, the railroad crossing guard bells clanging out of tune. The wind picks up and rushes through the trees, raising and lowering limbs, leaves spiral all about, hail crunches into metal, huge rain drops scatter the buds of flowers, branches splinter, shingles take flight off of roofs. The gutters on houses overflow and water splashes into guttural puddles of deep, rich mud. The air is dark as midnight at two in the afternoon, then, suddenly, there are no birds.

This is when the unconscious moves in and creation takes control. Hidden secrets might shine forth at this point, you never know. A glimpse of the impossible appears in a spark of bright lightning. It is the time when creative forces come forth in spontaneity, when all the world's a rattle and, for an artist (which we all are without knowing it), this chaos, this darkness, these fears are unconsciously craved. There is nothing better than witnessing the rational world being shredded to bits since it allows us to look at the world with new eyes. It allows us to verify that caring about creation, spontaneity and uncertainty are worth a life's efforts. Renewal and creation is all consuming. As Rilke said of a person who knows that their calling is to be creative, "only be attentive to that which rises up in you and set it above everything that you observe about you. What goes on in your innermost being is worthy of your whole love." If the whale comes by and swallows you, love that. If the tornado spins you and pulls you and wrenches open honey hidden inside a tree, cherish that moment, use that, create, understand and live with individualized and unique feelings, thoughts and insights even if they seem to mean nothing at all except they just seem right. Especially hold them dear if they first seem at odds with the moral majority. Hold your ear to the ground as a storm goes away; listen to the rainwater seeping into the earth, consult the rumble of a distant thunder clap as the storm drifts to the southeast.

When does the storm really end? It doesn't. The clouds and the wind and sirens all stop, but when the sun breaks through and illuminates the earth, well, it might be that this is part of the color I am looking for, am praying for. Any thoughts that have arrived cling and stay and integrate. For some people this amounts to accumulation and wisdom, maybe even mystical insight as though tromping the desert in mystic contemplation.

The storm has left a mark: a red cedar tree has split open and golden, halo-esque cedar sap is floating, drifting as a cloud above a single spot on the earth. I reach out and eat, sniff in with strong inhalence this golden cloud of sap. Right there above this cracked tree is pure air, a smell similar to that of a just born baby. I am first drawn to it from out of the corner of my eye as though a star. I don't doubt that this is the spot of some golden, virgin birth.

The tree already existed, but the spirit that finds rise is newly released. There is sticky real resin coming from the wood, dripping in globs and I touch it and it sticks. Good. I taste it, no words for that. There are no wild and extraordinary dimensions to any of it, just flat, simple, existence in the instant at peace. I soak this color up and feel added to, somehow more complete with the world where I live. I consider that I have deepened my accord with this always brave new world. Am struck with the insight of the bold and heroic Saint Emo. I wonder why humans are always going at destroying and conquering the world.

Now is the storm over? No. There are still the confessions and prayers that all of us made when the wind increased, when the air turned green, when the tree limb came plunging down by our garage. Do we really stand by those wishes, probably not. But there is a sense of strength gained all the same. For a brief moment everyone transcended themselves, went beyond their jobs and tasks and group mindthink. There was a brief period of time when we were not thinking about the safety of ourselves, our partners, our houses, didn't care whether the power went off; we were all just following the lightning bolt's jagged, splintering patterns in the dark day sky, watching as trees twisted, bent and from time to time crunched to the ground. There was a moment when we only heard the wind, only heard the thunder and were so utterly captivated that we were lost within the world of the wild and natural instantaneousness. Were in that place of nowhere, or perhaps that realm of anywhere at anytime, at the center of the entire universe. This sort of unconsciousness sets all of us free.

While the winds whipped and the thunder bloated we all wondered absurdly, are those bowling balls cutting down pins up there in the sky, or considered if we were hearing giant cottonwood trees howling to coyotes? These thoughts melt through and out of each person as the sun reappears and the wind dies down. It is true, yes, what happened did happen, what thoughts were thought really were thought. Childish worries, thoughts, fears perhaps, but they were real all the same.

There's more still. Listless, pondering, staggering, everyone moves to the outdoors in speechless wonder. Trees settle down. Dogs end their pacing and sniff the air, maybe lie down with a humpf. Birds flitter one by one back into flocks. There are a few obvious things that everyone is drawn to. Someone standing next to you might say, "Did you see that tree fall?" You'll say you did. Next your fears will return, a brief shiver up your neck. Then your hopes will briefly sparkle. Then you'll remember yourself, your passions, your children, think about what could have happened, might have happened. Most of the time though it turns out that things are still okay, different, but you and yours survived. Now, the storm is over, at least until you lay down sometime soon and it enters your dreams and that place where all tornadoes and whales and oceans dwell.

4.

There is always sky though, even after a storm is past. The world on the plains is mostly above you and what happens up there is anyone's guess. Such blatancy is easy to lament as though it was a lost life time during your childhood years. (Have you looked at a picture of yourself around age ten recently, does that person still exist in you? Or is it now a memorial cloud drifting high and far, laughing lostly in the wind). There are those who are grown up in the standard sense of the word, yet declare they'll never be happy again, at least not happy again like they were as a kid. There are people who have somehow or another just become lost and scared and for whatever reason never develop the courage to live a full ranging life of luck, failure, success, joy, sorrow, love and anger. Just can't overcome fear and instead opt for a rather sad feeling of continual, but empty, isolated satisfaction.

Losing control of yourself is easy. One day you look up in the sky and wonder what you're doing driving forty minutes to work where you'll be trying to sell magazines, or raise money for the Republican party, where you'll be trying to peddle travel packages endorsed by some second rate celebrity. You'll wonder if it's true: will I be stuck at this pitiful job until I retire? What happened to me along the way. Why am I sitting here listening to someone complain to me about their cable television bill, threatening me with bodily harm over the sports station, a boxing match? What must be even worse is if you went to college, went to trade school, sacrificed time and money, ego and yet more time to get the job you have, in fact tried hard to get, yet now feel cheated, or duped, or are too embarrassed to try and change because it turns out that you wanted a certain type of job, or house, or car, or coat because you thought it was supposed to be the right one according to others, but now that you have it are not satisfied. When this happens just keep looking up to the sky for an answer. Drift and discover where the answers have gone, are going. Most importantly toss the time table you've got in your brain out the window. Just because you didn't reach point B according to the time schedule of Mr. and Mrs. Jones doesn't mean life is over. Expectations can be your worst nightmare, but are also what may lead you to your savior!

A large majority of Midwesterners hate where they live and what they've become. So they sit wishing for mountains and waterfalls, oceans and beaches, bears and sharks. As a result people become immersed in insurance and television, in dreams of escape and exotic cruise vacations, envious of those "freaks" who live out in California. They miss the glory of where they already are. Waiting for something important to happen, or worse yet, sit convinced nothing ever will happen in their flat, plain, boring little town called Nowheresville.

Many of you have seen the sad people I'm speaking of in your town—they plod along, miserable citizens overburdened with chores of tedium, their faces look like they might split in half if a smile crossed it. Maybe you've witnessed them as ravenous tourists though, clinging and erratic, short-fused and sarcastic as though chained animals set free, believing they should have everything they want, living as though they have one week in their lives a year. And who can blame them in some ways, after all, they have suffered by-God and now they're on vacation, so move aside and give them instant pleasure, sacrifice for them as they have for their employers. These starving people are never free though. They spend a good portion of their vacations answering their cell phone and talking to their kids who want to borrow money. They drive around the affluent parts of the town they're visiting fantasizing about buying a vacation house with a beautiful view, or sit around wondering what they would be doing now if they were at work. To me they seem like that ever-famous line in Sinclair Lewis' Babbitt, "I have never done a single thing I've wanted to my whole life." This is such a sobering reflection on how people often find themselves. It seems important to ask yourself if this is happening to you.

In Iowa, people honestly believe and are taught that if you were really any good at anything you'd be living in New York, Boston, Atlanta, California, Paris, with a view of the mountains, or at least in Chicago where *important* things happen. If you're any good you certainly wouldn't be living in a place like Tipton, Iowa, or some other small Midwestern village like Viroqua, or Preston.

The value of the land isn't addressed, the potentials of the earth, the seasons, the local environment's spirit to inspire artwork all ignored. It would be so easy to twist all this around. People could just decide not to move, to care about where they live, could start making wood kiln caves and throwing pottery. There is a true feeling of greatness I feel when I walk into a person's basement and see canned vegetables lined up in rows. This sort of effort is truly bigger and grander than the city of New York. People could shift their faith to the land and have faith in what they can do, not what others do, or what large corporate media sources propose we ought to be doing for them.

I would have loved this sort of thing when I was little. It would have been so cool if instead of taking field trips to see displays at the museum which centered on animals from Africa, or reptiles of the Galapagos Islands, if we had been taken to a Cloud Watching Museum, or visited a truly happy dairy farmer, talked with an organic gardener. I can't imagine the horizon's which might have been opened inside me if I had been taken to see a local artist's studio full of rocks, bark, barn wood, corn, the seeds of Iowa. I am nearly ashamed to admit I had no idea that a person could study art in college during my first four years of school. Not to be inspired by and taught the wealth of where you live is a total waste and completely disrespectful to those brave people who have come before us and who have created fully meaningful, exciting, imaginative lives here in Iowa, about Iowa, or Wisconsin, or Minnesota.

At this point in our society there is nothing more important that needs to be done than disregarding the New York's and Los Angeles's and Chicago's and declaring you are going to take your zest and zeal and talents back where you first learned about life, where your inspirations were truly hatched and bring them (often times back) to life. I believe that if you really want to develop as a person, if you really want to know a place, want to experience real whole hearted success, then take your words and imagination back where you first walked and played as a child, or at least go where you feel you "grew up." This is what building a community really means after all. Paul Gruchow, a Minnesotan, suggests that the literal meaning of community is, "a group of people who have made together the rite of passage from adolescence to adulthood."

I agree with Mr. Gruchow. Contribute to the past, the present and the future for real! This is not only rewarding, but mythic, involving you in an initiation rite. This idea isn't some new fangled thing that looms impossibly doomed to failure. Wes Jackson who lives in Salina, Kansas and runs the Land Institute speaks of having college students major in "homecoming." It's rather sad that this is all considered no more than dreaming, however. In my talks with decent and caring college students these days ninety nine percent of them don't care about Iowa, don't care about their hometowns, are even slightly embarrassed by the place they were raised as a kid. In fact, even if they wanted to stay they have been raised to leave. Of course, the ones who do stay are thought to be rather strange and low achievers.

Unfortunately Iowans will continue to run toward jiggy, jittery dreams of oceans, uselessly peaking mountains, rotten and faulty big cities which suck down energy. What's worse, our state taxes and minds wholeheartedly support this, we grant money to students, to faculty, to politicians to go elsewhere, to work for people in different lands and think that by tying ourselves to "causes" beyond Iowa we are somehow more important for it. Many of our local ministries and volunteer groups reach out not to people in their midst, but to causes in South America, or Florida, seemingly anywhere but here, as though thinking globally was of some greater value to those they live next to. This is as dumb to me as sending food to Africa when the people in your own town, county, or state are starving and mistreated.

It seems perplexing to me to think that there are creative artists trying to make a difference in the Midwest, trying to create and understand this place we could all call home, yet because they aren't called Doctors, or Lawyers can't muster up a living wage. It's no secret, most parents hope their kids can move out into the important places of the world, not for a second thinking that where they live ought to be the most important place there is. Don't think what this says about themselves.

I can't claim to have been any better of course. When I first understood where I lived instead of cherishing it, I quested to escape and wanted a rocky mountain high. I remember standing atop a park bench in downtown Iowa City and thinking I had to get out, needed to leave this foolish, limiting, pathetic town of insignificance so that I could be somebody. I wish I could say that I am a better person for having left. This is the way everyone wants things to work anyway. To think that you've seen the world and are better for it is the popular, liberal-posing and affluent way of looking at the world and since so many do move I suppose it is necessary to believe that moving is good, but just because something is done doesn't mean it is of quality.

I'll admit, I have learned about one perspective, but I won't know if this is correct or not. A person can't fully understand a place if they ever leave, and perhaps vice versa. Just as one can't claim to know marriage better because you've been divorced. You can't because you don't know the parts pertaining to continuing a marriage. Of course, you can't know marriage completely just because you've always been married either, since without it you can't completely understand it, but the secrets in this staying married thing are becoming less and less known and more mysterious all the time aren't they. I remember talking with one of my friends one day and thinking that it was so uncool that we each had parents whom hadn't been divorced. There seems to be some social status, some brownie points awarded to people who can start a story about themselves with, "My parents were divorced when I was ... "

These days what could be more radical and misunderstood than staying married to the same person forever and continuing to live in the town you grew up in and what's more, enjoying it and even more radical yet, being wildly and passionately proud of yourself!

Haste and greatness are symptoms of the modern mind. So many people are searching for the incredible, the stunning, the best, the most unique and at such speeds that they miss the most obvious method of enlightenment: roots and contemplation. Exaggeration is often a trick used by people to seem better than others, to come across as better than they are. Things are so strange that people assume everything everyone's doing is motivated by the quest to be great and right. Some people declare after living somewhere for six, seven months that they have somehow arrived at their home, but home is more than a declaration, it takes time no matter the feelings you may have.

Change is a healer, not something that ought to be avoided. How do you really know if you can maintain your belief in a *God*, or *The Way* if you give up on your individualized sense of God? Perhaps only by continuing to work with prayers, by examining other types of prayer, by better understanding the flow of creek water, by studying and putting credence in what you distrust and not feeling that you've sinned because you don't automatically and always carry your belief all the time. Patience and commitment as well as a sense of wonder and doubt are the best tools we have to know anything.

Do you want to experience a truly remarkable relationship with someone, then stay with them. Who does that? Why don't things seem right these days? If you were to ask the late-mythologist Joseph Campbell he'd tell you people aren't following their bliss, but more immediate concerns and ideas outside themselves such as money and fame, denying themselves things that are important to themselves, yet claim they have no time for, insisting that their dreams are not the sort of activity that "adults," do. There is a dramatic line between being busy with work and busily working on what you want to do. What's the next sentence Babbitt says after the before mentioned one? "I don't know's I've accomplished anything except get along." O such pitiful comments, the self imposed tired life.

How often do most of us put off the things that we think are the most important because we have placed a series of more immediate, but actually unimportant tasks in our way. We may think exercising and writing are vitally important, yet put them off and off and off in order to do some trivial task denying ourselves what we really want, thinking we'll get to the "good" things later, once we get caught up with the bosses requests, with the yardwork, etc. We end up putting things off so long that the sign in the tavern that reads, *"Free Beer Tomorrow"* is no longer funny, but the saddest cruelest thought of all.

People like to feel sorry for themselves though. I often get the feeling that people thrive on incompetence and depression. Are lazy because it allows them to fail. Seems like many people want to make things hard. A hard worker is a good person we are always told. Think about some of those well educated people in your life, they think they know everything, talk and talk and talk as if the world depended on what they have to say, yet these people can't even cook an egg, can't clean out a gutter, can't get dirty. They can't face the thought of catching a fish, certainly couldn't eat wild blackberries in the forest, although they would pay extravagant prices for organic berries at their local market. Selective incompetence, fear, denial who knows what it's all about. People are incompetent because for some reason it works and enables them to then become lazy and then I would guess sad. Writer Jim Harrison states in a story of his, "The danger of civilization, of course, is that you will piss away your life on nonsense."

So what's to be made of the clouds in the sky? Watch them, meditate. Wish upon stars. Notice the moon waxing and waning. Wonder to yourself how slow can you move and still be fully alive.

What have I learned from having moved away from Iowa and then coming back? I've learned that what you see is definitely not what you get. That there is good and bad everywhere. That dreams are true, but need a heap of that old fashioned elbow grease to become vitalized. That you need to know what you want to get it, but that you have to go with the flow and accept what just happens in order to get there, have to believe that there is some hidden force that will guide and move you in the right direction if you are being true to yourself. You have to accept that what you love the most can cause you the most pain of all. That nothing is right and that people who have given up on finding spirituality are lost because in my mind they have given up on creativity.

I've learned that if you can't merge your past with the present and see into the future you're stunted badly. I learned that there are drunks everywhere. That there are loud pickup trucks everywhere. But there aren't passages into confidence, aren't places where you can stand and remember laughter fifteen years ago everywhere you go. Without feeling competent in a non-doubting way about yourself, you'll never really know what you want. I believe that feeling part of everything happens from where you have come of age, this doesn't mean that I can't take these things with me and live somewhere else, but if I do I will be losing part of who I am and this idea should never be taken lightly.

I've learned that what I thought was naïve isn't. That most of what I've been told by people I thought of as adults and teachers isn't true, but part of a big mind scam based on marketing and an affluent moral system, mostly created by a greedy few that have convinced a majority of people to follow along with the threat of something along the lines of unemployment, or being reincarnated as a piece of burned charcoal. I've learned that how much you can realize of your imagination is vital. That caring about your quality of life and how it effects the actual place you live is of the utmost importance. Once again, to quote Lao-Tzu, "Benefit comes from what is there; Usefulness comes from what is not." (v.11)

5.

Being born is an innocent and naïve proposition. Naïve existence changes as adults try and remove a child's independent and freshly original view of life. Of course, being naïve is not something you are aware of while growing up. How naïve was I? I didn't even know cuss words until second grade. I honestly didn't know they existed, or what they were. I discovered them from Dean and Scott, a couple of farm kids I befriended when I started second grade at a new school. These two were great, they taught me how to draw football helmets too.

Even though I tried to be an imaginative child I was never quite able to live as boldly as I might have because I was also very literal. I don't suppose anyone is much different. I built forts with my friends, enjoyed causing trouble with cars that drove by our house, liked making homemade cigarettes with dried mint and notebook paper, had firecrackers blow up in my hand, played football, made treehouses, had lemonade stands, went swimming … being as kids are, free and fully alive, I'd even say wild, at each moment.

As far as I remember we never thought about things like miracles in my neighborhood. I'm sure we had all been told about various Gods and creation.

We knew all about holidays, but personally I didn't even comprehend the full story of Christmas except that it was fun to see people in a good mood and sometimes we went to visit my grandparents down in Texas. I don't know that we needed miracles to tell you the truth, or rather, I think there's a good chance that we figured everything was a miracle in my pack of friends.

In the continual effort to have fun we tested the limits of what we considered possible. Our miracles arrived as surprises, from things like owls and tadpoles, mudballs, tobaggon jumps, while searching around in old junk yards and riding our skateboards on vertical walls. Many things didn't register with me as a kid though. Take cold weather for instance. I remember playing football in the snow for a whole day, literally, then as night came, going home and being bewildered that my feet were numb. Then scared when they became unbearably hot. I jumped into bed and hoped the feelings would go away. Or another time I remember drinking two quarts of pickle juice and wondering why three hours into sleep I woke up gagging and puking. My world was shaped by surprises and extremes, not by miracles. I didn't understand the meanings of creativity then, I just took advantage of its natural existence.

I remember that one of my buddies father was a preacher, but to me and my other friends the only thing this meant was that we couldn't cuss around him, or dare utter the word *God*, which we sometimes did in our lives when we wanted to express extreme amazement, it was truly a synonym for Wow! Awesome! Spectacular! I vaguely remember that we didn't utter the word God in this man's presence though because there was a chance that he had the power to relay our actions to the real God, who upon hearing about our outlandish behavior would consider us bad kids and in need of some harsh discipline soon, or perhaps in the afterlife. Of course, if we weren't caught then there was no problem, we wouldn't be sent to hell.

Naturally, I didn't have a completely firm idea what this place called hell was all about either. I knew it was bad, but not really why, or who was in charge, or why the only way to this place was by saying particular words, or by acting in ways that adults thought of as bad. That hell was supposed to be beneath the ground, where we dug around seemed odd as well.

At one point in my life I might have found hell though. I had embarked on a rather common adventure with one my friends. We had procured a foldable army shovel and declared that we would dig to China. We made pretty good progress too, we were down to our knees after one afternoon. As we got ready to leave we seriously considered a variety of questions: What would have happen when we made it to China? What would happen if it turned out that hell really was halfway between here and China? It's not that I didn't think the earth could contain a place under the ground such as hell, I just wondered where it was and if we would disturb it on our trip through the earth.

6.

So many thoughts as a child. Sometimes I wonder who I am? Wonder when I began to lose my childhood? I've hinted at some things already. I'll try and tell a little more.

I was born in 1963 so according to popular news magazines I am one of the last of the Baby Boomers, therefore I must not be part of Gen X. I can assure you I have no idea what either of these categories mean so probably I am not part of either, or if I am I wouldn't claim to be. I have always agreed with Woody Allen, who said something along the lines of, "I'd never join a group that would have me as one of its members."

I came to life in a hospital somewhere in downtown Detroit less than a week after President Kennedy was assassinated in Dallas. I am an adopted child, and I've been told, not directly by my parents, that I went through two other sets of parents first. The fact that I have heard this from others is typical, people will often tell others things that they may never say to the ones that it might mean the most to. Whenever I read that adopted children have not had proper bonding with parents I wonder if that's true or not. I look at my own tiny daughter and know that good things are happening because my wife and I are holding her, listening to her early on in her life. However, when I think about myself floating from place to place early in life I understand that there's nothing I can do about the past so I don't concern myself with the ramifications of a bumpy early childhood. In some circles of people I am considered fine, so things must have worked out okay. I have never wished to know anything about my genetic parents in my life which may seem surprising, but not to me.

My family moved from Michigan to Iowa when I was about two, maybe two and a half. I lived in true delight without real worries in Iowa until I reached seventh grade, at which time I discovered there were three things of importance. Two of them, girls and social events, I was not well suited to because I was too shy and scared to open my mouth. I rarely said anything to anybody other than a few friends. I was also surprised at how much taller and bigger other people were. One of my friends and I, who was my size, determined that everyone else was so big because they ate large quantities of candy and gobs and gobs of cheese-flavored corn chips.

The third thing of importance involved sports and I was well suited to this. I did them all with an aggressive and blind passion: football, basketball, track, baseball, skateboarding, biking. These activities came easily to me. I truly enjoyed sports during junior high school. I participated with such blind enthusiasm that I am confused about it. I am bewildered that I am unable to sit down and tell you a good-hearted, inspiring sports stories from my life. What all my adventures in sports meant I still don't know. I do know that I wasn't very coachable and so didn't always do what was asked of me, even if this meant not starting, or playing quarterback, or point guard. I had a belief that I knew more than the coaches most of the time and was stubborn to the point of depression.

I also tried to be a musician. I owned a trombone and signed up for band. This interest went all right in eighth and ninth grade, but in seventh grade myself and one other kid, Chuck Truebrook, who wanted to play the trumpet, were so awful, so out of tune, so bad that even over a hundred others playing instruments couldn't cover us up. We were banished from the group and told to practice apart from the band, in a room at the end of a hallway during first period. This seclusion didn't help us get any better, however. We never dared to play loud enough that anyone might hear us. I mean we knew we were awful and laughter was the only sensible cure.

Other things became clear about life in that hallway though. We got visits from the "hoods." When I first started school at Central Junior High I was wholeheartedly terrified of these people. They smoked and dressed in ratty and what I imagined must be smelly, oily clothing. I had never seen anything like them. My Uncles and Aunts smoked, but for some reason it became them much easier in their tiny rural Texas homes than it did these kids who were supposedly close to my age.

Certainly no one I knew was a hood. My friends and I had experimented with smoking, we were by no means innocent, but when we did something we believed to be "wrong" we did our best to hide, or cover our actions up. We never would have dreamt of hanging out, smoking and trying to look mean at school, in front of adults and teachers. Never.

Anyway, while me and Chuck sat in the hallway during first period and were supposed to be practicing our band music we had occasions to talk with these hoods, who were skipping class I guess, and they were actually pretty funny. Corky, the leader of the hoods, was quite overweight. He dressed in faded denim pants, some sort of fading Armed Forces t-shirt and a matching, faded denim jacket with patches sewn on it. He wore a tattered looking engineer cap perched slightly back on his curly haired head as well. His clothing and the black leather boots he wore made him look more like an adult to my eyes than a ninth grader. He had an independent attitude, yet he wasn't really very frightening at all once I got to know him. In fact, Corky seemed rather compassionate and gentle. It turned out he liked talking about comic books and cartoons, especially some character named Sgt. Rock who he seemed to idolize. Corky would also talk about his dad that had been in the Marines, or about various farts he had let off in study hall and how he got a kick out of watching the faces of the girls around him when the smell drifted their way. One morning he told us how he'd just made-out with one of the "chicks" across the street. Then he laughed at me when my face turned bright red. Chuck and me would laugh right along with him most of the time. I wouldn't say that Corky became a friend of mine, but I wasn't sacred of him anymore and in fact I began to like hearing his stories.

I also experienced my first adult that seemed to break some unspoken bond I thought existed between all other adults in that hallway room. The building janitor, Lewis, would always hold his ears when he walked by us and laugh. He was the only adult in the building who ever smiled it seemed to me. The teachers and the hall monitors and office workers all looked constipated and serious, as if some disaster was about to happen at any moment. They all looked as though life were some inconsiderate burden they had to survive without crying.

Sometimes Lewis would come in, sit down and talk to us. Well, I knew that people worked for money, and that everyone was different, but still, I hadn't actually heard an adult complain about their job, or express disrespect about others before. Lewis thought the same teachers me and Chuck considered morons were as well. Previous to this, I must have figured that all adults were content with their jobs and never made fun of each other. The things Lewis said about the teachers: what they had in their desks, the way they acted in the teacher's lounge when the students weren't around for instance just didn't seem possible to me. He went on about the teachers who fussed over their hair styles in the men's room, how often and long they went to the restrooms, how most of them actually hated their students and even teaching. He told us who had problems with alcohol, who took drugs. Lewis even told us that some of the teachers were having affairs with other teachers at the school. I seemed to have been more shocked than Chuck about this since he started laughing before I did. Lewis definitely made me look at adults and many of my teachers in a completely different way.

Obviously we were some of the worst musicians of all-time to grace Central Junior High. Lewis told us he'd never known the band teacher to ever relegate anyone to the hallway in his nearly thirty-five years of employment, but he added that he kind of liked us being here. The next two years we got to sit with the rest of the band, but to tell you the truth I kind of missed people like Corky and Lewis. There were good stories going on behind the scenes.

In my years of public education I was mostly numb to learning. I was not by any means a scholarly student. I was either incapable, or unwilling to memorize anything not to mention unable to pay attention, or take an interest in what was told to me. For some reason I thought almost everything was stupid. I was a C^+ student. No matter how hard I tried, or didn't try I got C^+'s. I couldn't understand it. In fact, what usually happened was that the harder I tried the worse I did.

I'll never forget when I tried really hard on the reading test in 4th grade. I thought through every answer completely, going over all the multiple choice possibilities in my mind. The harder I thought things out though the more none of the answers seemed right to me. Feeling completely lost I managed to test into the lowest reading group, which completely and absolutely devastated me. I tried to talk my way out of this situation, pleading with my teacher, begging my parents to speak with my teacher, but nothing worked. I was thoroughly shocked and disgusted with the adults around me. I could literally read so much better than the others in my new group. It was embarrassing to be sitting in a circle with the kids my friends and I had all thought of as the idiots. That no one thought it was a mistake for me to be sitting with these kids seemed at once both preposterous and horribly frightening.

The fact that I wasn't given a chance to explain the answers I had picked on my reading test really upset me. I should have been allowed to prove myself. I was stuck though. For some reason, from that day forward I was no longer picked for any of the school activities that I considered normal for people in my grade. I was left out of the 5th grade social studies group, left out of the 6th grade reading and study group. I had to be in gym classes with kids in lower grades, had to be in music and art with younger kids. I remember being more than angry. I remember feeling helpless and invisible. I just couldn't understand it. What had I done? I knew I wasn't stupid, but apparently I could never demonstrate this to the right people. What did I do? Well, I stopped trying of course.

I quit doing my assigned weekly goals which caused me to be grounded and isolated in my classroom, but I didn't care. After awhile I was grounded so often that the rules weren't enforced. I didn't know it then, but I now know that I felt betrayed by the adults around me. I felt equal to anyone, but was being treated as an inferior person, never being challenged, or respected, just pushed aside. I was so upset that the poor teacher must have become scared as I was constantly being kept after school for bad behavior. My parents were even called in to hear about my "glaring" insubordinate manners. I wasn't alone in this though. As luck would have it, one of my friends was also considered a trouble maker, or some sort of a threat to this teacher. For some reason though he wasn't put in the lowest reading group which was somewhat perplexing to me at the time since this meant that it wasn't my behavior that was causing me to be in the low reading group, but possibly, and this was the really scary part, maybe I really was just stupid.

If there was something wrong with me I guess I'll never know. Once you stop trusting adults like I did, then any efforts that occur on your behalf are not taken seriously. So when I was told that I would be working with a tutor to learn my vowels I was totally bewildered, but said nothing. What did this tutoring consist of? I sat in some ladies kitchen and said the letters *a e i o u* and *y*, over and over again, as short sounds and long sounds. It was practically worthless, but I did get a piece of candy at the end of each session. Recently I discovered that many religious chants are based on emitting the full range and utterance of vowel sounds, so maybe I was being raised to be a wise man, or Gregorian chanter. Honestly though, after awhile I felt more like a spy than a student being held back. I remember taking the time to observe the adults and their tricks to try and help me. I was conscious that the adults were wrong about me and I went along with it while at school which wasn't hard to do. I just took the easy way out of everything because I could. Nothing was expected out of me.

Having decided that there was no harm in being completely unchallenged, I just started to sit around and watch what was going on. Smiling in the face of my declared inadequacies. I never enjoyed knowing I was missing out on the things my friends got to do though: the reports and the science projects they were involved with seemed like fun to me, even exciting, but what could I do, apparently my life was no longer in my hands so I pretended not to care.

I was continually amazed though. My supposed inadequacies never seemed to end. I was told I needed handwriting tutoring in 5th grade. I was appalled. I was sent to the school library with a volunteer tutor to practice my letters. I never intended to write in cursive anyway I declared, the adults told me I would. I was told my lowercase K's were illegible, so I drew out five hundred of them in a row on specially lined paper that looked like lanes of interstate highway. Then it turned out I needed spelling tutoring. Then it was determined that maybe I had an attitude problem and was offered a series of Pavlovian rewards for acting nice to the teachers.

Half of 4th grade and all through 5th and 6th grade I had a university student who came to our school especially to work with me on reading and writing. Once again, I couldn't figure it out. I knew my vowels didn't I?! This student tutor would help me with reading and sentence structure, asking me where periods should go to clean up run-on sentences. Things I was willing to do when, or if, I felt like it, but what was the point if you'd have asked me then. I charmed him by making sure I had some writing errors that we could go over together and correct each week. I'll never forget the outrage expressed by both the tutor and my teacher when I failed to do a writing sample one week. The nerve of it, this university student came in only to help me with writing and I had failed miserably once again. "Geezz," I remember thinking, "it's not like either of you think I'm smart or anything, who cares if I forgot." In my mind I was being failed by teachers every day of my life.

On days when I did have writing to go over we would conclude each session with him doing various tests on me: holding ink blobs in front of me to see what I saw. He'd show me pictures of houses and kids on swings and ask where I'd like to be in the photo. He had all sorts of these tests he put me through. I guess I never passed any of these tests since I continued to have to meet with him and he continued to put tests in front of me until I left to go on to Junior High. In the early days of these tests I thought everyone was doing them, but, of course, it turned out it was just me.

I used to hate the moment my personal tutor arrived. Everyone would watch me walk out and then watch me come back in the classroom. There might as well of been a large neon sign that said there goes the stupid idiot! All along I just knew that I didn't have any problems. I just couldn't. How could I. In my real life, when I was outside playing, talking, living with other kids my age I was fine. I had good friends and they never ever hinted to me that I was stupid, couldn't read, couldn't write. None of them ever treated me as though I were inadequate that I remember. I could write as well as they could, understood math as well as they did during summer vacation. I just never suspected that I was in any way lacking in ability. I seriously doubt if I did lack any. To this day I can't explain why all these tests and tutors were part of my life.

Something about me made teachers uneasy and I have never understood what it was, probably never will. I know now that independent thinking is the most feared trait of all organized groups so my guess is I didn't go along as quietly as expected. If you'd have asked anyone that knew me in school what I'd end up doing when I turned 35 they never would have thought I'd be a writer. I was probably written off as another ho-hum person.

Apparently there were fairly low expectations for me. I'll never forget being the lead customer service employee at a local cable company and telling my dad I was going to quit. He wondered why I would leave such a great job. "Wasn't I good at it?" he asked me. I was stunned, wanting to say, "Surely you don't think this is my lot in life, surely I haven't met your expectations? You can't look at me and think these are my dreams fulfilled!" When he stated this though I suddenly understood a lot of what happened to me in life, low expectations come true easy. I understand that there is nothing wrong with any job that a person does for money, and would never dream of mocking anothers hard efforts at life. However, only a fool couldn't have seen, or understood my passions in life and understand that being a customer service representative wasn't related to the long journey ahead, especially if it didn't need to be.

Of course this is probably another thing that bothered teachers and adults about me: my ability to ignore the obvious and the real in favor of my efforts to try and defy the improbable. I have always agreed with writer Edward Abbey, I just haven't known it all the time, "There is a way of being wrong, which is also sometimes necessarily right."

I will admit though, I probably am one of the worst students that has ever graduated from an institution of higher learning. It's really a travesty that I have a graduate degree! I learned what I wanted to, no more, sometimes less. Considering I ended up with an English degree and went through a graduate program in Secondary English Education and have no idea what the parts of sentence consist of is proof, believe me. I know nothing about grammar, I'm not proud of it, but there you have it. Believe it or not it was never taught, or at least not in any class I ever had. Throughout college I only gave answers according to what I thought was right, not in accordance with what was professed to me in class. I guess this is being stubborn, but I preferred to believe I was harboring ideals and having independent opinions, engaging in the act of learning. Since it was my decision to go to school and money was paid to do so, I rationalized that this seemed fair. Much to my surprise this was not the way it was. Yet, for some reason, at some point during college I stopped being a C+ student and began to be an A student. I have no idea why.

Perhaps I started getting better grades because I was resolved to believe in myself finally. To cast away my doubts of being inadequate. To quit straddling what was expected and proper with what I thought was right.

What does it really take to be an adult in our current society. The minimum standard seems to be that you can go in debt. That you are able to create bills in your name, that you have a bank account, probably a credit card helps. Usually this involves living away from your parents. It ought to mean that you can accept what decisions you make as your own and not blame others. That you stand in line and wait your turn. That you can avoid judging everyone else as better or worse than you. That you have a way of contributing to society. One hopes it entails that you aren't still trying to please only your parents. That you are able to take care of yourself. That you can deal with making hard decisions, can do things that you don't like to do and be happy anyway. Hopefully it means doing what makes you happy and carving out a way to live as you please despite the annoying tasks and opinions and obstacles that get in your way.

I believe one of the primary ways to know if you are an adult is if you are able to control your imagination and "seriousness" at appropriate times. That is, can you pretend to be "grown up" when you need to be? Can you see through all the petty manners and polite bits of protocol? Can you smile about performing regimented table manners? Can you hold down a job when need be, not spend money when you don't have it? Can you feed yourself without slowly becoming malnourished over time, (I mean years, not just a day or two)? Can you meet deadlines and accomplish tasks you set out for yourself. Can you suffer setbacks with a resolve to continue forward, disregarding fear and greed. Do you appreciate new ideas and understand the importance of physical activity and not just playing mind games all day and night? Do you honestly believe that there are an infinite number of honorable ways to live a good life? Do you find time to engage in your passions, do you have passions aside from work? Do you care about your house, your city, township, place on this earth?

Often times one becomes an adult in rather embarrassing ways. I did, that's for certain. I'll never forget the first poetry contest I entered in college. I was a senior and had spent the summer evenings after my job as a tropical fish packer working on a poem which was one hundred and seven pages long entitled, *Water Color Writings*. I truly believed that I had formulated what would eventually be one of literatures enduring and respected masterpieces. I felt I had merged sight and sound with smell and taste, had created a reality that would answer all questions anyone had of life. At first I thought I wouldn't enter the poetry contest, it wouldn't be fair, I mean, was the faculty and staff in Kansas ready? Heck was the world ready, for what I had written? Would the truths I had so clearly, so deeply exposed be too big an expanse on human understanding at one time? Keep in mind, I was serious about this. I really and truly believed I had cracked through to some grand and previously elusive understandings of life and spirit. I had poured my heart and soul into this poem and once shared, I was certain would shatter and blow others away. I had sacrificed going out with friends, playing basketball, even more or less giving up my dreams of being a college-level teacher so that I could be a poet and a writer. I had sat in my one room apartment with a manual typewriter, secluded, writing what I was certain would soon become an incredible contribution to human knowledge and literature.

When the deadline approached in December I decided I would enter my creation and claim the prize, ending my life as I knew it for fame and literary glory. I reminded myself that I would have to remember to stay a humble poet of the people and not one of those famous tea sipping, mock-elitist who lost their roots with the first glimmer of cash. The winner was to be announced March 15th and I decided I would be ready.

Well, I knew it would take a few days for the letter to reach me declaring my victory. By April 5th I thought I better go check and make sure there hadn't been some sort of confusion, perhaps the jurors had lost my address. I walked in to the English Department office, asked about the poetry contest and the secretary said the winners had been announced a couple weeks ago. He pointed to a tattered handout taped out in the hallway. I simply nodded my head and strolled over to take a look at my name on the list.

Suddenly it occurred to me as my eyes glanced over the list of winners that I hadn't won. Not even an honorable mention. I was completely devastated. Running off like a frightened kid into the woods near campus and agonized in tears for hours in stunned and pitiful disbelief and agony. This was not possible, the judges must not have taken the time to really understand what I had submitted, it must have been a mistake. How could my greatness be denied?! It was an outrage, a conspiracy, a plot to deny me my place as a writer in the world. Didn't they know what I sacrificed? Didn't they know greatness when it was near them? Surely they had made a mistake!

I went tail spinning into a depression over what I considered to be the injustice of this contest and then decided I must be some sorry sap failure and that I would never amount to diddly squat. I was literally heart broken since the best I felt I could offer to the world was apparently of no consequence, even unimportant. I would begin to walk to class from my apartment and as I approached campus I would begin to cry and sob. I refused to believe that my ideas of the world weren't in synch with others. Alas, a change was needed, but I was unprepared. I had swerved too far into the realm of the neurotic. I was questing membership in a group of elite writers, trying too hard to be like some image I had of the poets I admired. Believed that I deserved something which I really didn't.

Once the depression wore off, with the help of medication and counseling I came to the realization that I hadn't failed, wasn't a stupid person or anything else along those lines and instead accepted reality. Part of which included being proud of myself for what I wrote and not to be concerned about contests. I understood that I needed to avoid getting upset at other people and knowing that there was no conspiracy against me. I could either choose to keep writing, or not to. I understood that I needed to venture further into my journey through life and not let a small bump in the road swerve me from my hopes and dreams. If I was going to be a writer, I needed to understand that it was not going to be easy, or popular. I would have to give up many of the things I thought I would get in life such as tenure at a college with calming, regular paychecks and benefits.

I think this was a final passage into adulthood for me. Into independence. Not only did I come to accept my defeat, but at the same time I refused to quit writing. I resolved that I would write no matter what. So, in-between the many jobs I have gone through and probably will continue to go through, I write. I have come to understand that what you love the most can hurt you the most. This holds for all things, and all the people around me. I understand that if I am to love my daughter as much as I do, then I also need to be aware that she is capable of bringing me an incredible amount of pain. But one can't be scared to follow bliss and hope and dreams.

This determination to be a writer hasn't meant I know how to be an adult it just means I am not a child anymore. That is, I am free of being completely dependent on others, of needing the support of others to feel right. Now when I behave stupidly, I understand that it's just me being stupid, not the fault of some conspiring, cruel world. As for being an adult, that's always going on, longer than anyone's yet lived.

7.

Alan Watts says in his book The Wisdom of Insecurity, "Belief clings, faith lets go." I say, the world is mostly an invisible thing, but you'll need faith to justify this.

It sounds clever, but the invisible has been lost in our culture. For instance, when I was in Sitka, Alaska I walked through Totem Pole Park over and over again, more than thirty days in a row, almost always twice a day. Each time I felt confronted with an invisible force. The totem poles themselves were partly responsible, the clucks and barks and coos and rattles of the ravens were part of it, the cries and stares of the eagles, the peaking harbor seals part of it, as were the salmon bones along the shore and the tails of diving humpback whales, but the silence between the waves and the ravens, the space and light between the cedars and spruce, these were part too.

The only thing that could get in the way of sensing this invisible power was if I were to begin thinking I'd seen these totem poles before. If I began thinking that they were common place and if I thought I knew what was going on and quit examining, looking and wondering with them this would be tragic. It was important that I not let the totem poles become some rational thing that a park ranger simply figured out for me and left them at that.

Where that something in me that creates and registers awe and respect is I don't know. I can't and wouldn't want to identify this any further, it's not any different than the reverence one might have for trout when fly fishing, if you were able to fully understand why the fish break the surface of the water to snatch the fly when they do and how, if you could understand the thing completely then you'd be more inclined to stop as mystery and passion would be gone. Enjoying mystery, yet feeling in tune with the world is somewhere that only story and myth can deposit you. People often say poets write the music of the world, they do, but only if they write between the lines, and then only if we all go one step further and read between their lines.

To me it's important to respect and try to understand where you live. If you try to write about a sense of place while living three or four places at once, escaping winters by going south for instance, you won't ever understand where you live because you aren't experiencing all the place has to offer, or worse, don't want to appreciate all it has to offer. In fact I'd go so far as to suggest that moving constantly and/or leaving for whole seasons of the year indicates that you are incapable of appreciating any place since you can't love if you are harboring a portion of disdain for some parts.

I also can't figure out how people can just brush aside old Shamanic methods and long standing astrological hopes because the limits of science for instance can't verify these methods of understanding to be valid in rational, or empirical fashion.

I've already touched on the need for creativity, for faith, for mystery, for the invisible. How can it be meaningless that for centuries people have felt faith was enough? That icons reveal the truth to whole groups of people? That people have believed in the alignment of the stars for generations DOES make a difference.

To throw these sacred, traditional and important ways of knowing the world out the window in favor of reason and rationality and the scientific method is not only a mistake, but extremely dangerous. In a book by psychotherapist Gregory Max Vogt entitled Pathological Christianity he defines the goal of fundamentalism as that which, "is to control every single thought, feeling and behavior of every person on earth, and to own and command all the territory on earth." The seduction of science is the same as any other movement of tyrannical knowledge, it assures you of the truth and tries to offer a sense of security if you join the group. Then, if you do join, you'll no longer need to think or act for yourself, you just have to trust the agents of the truth who will do and solve and be everything for you. Wow, what a simple system, huh?!

I hate to be the one to let people in on this next bit of opinion, but if you need truth to feel secure, then you may need to look into procuring a different profession than that of human. I am stating these tenets of my belief with sincerity, with as much confidence as I can muster, yet the tricky part is that you totally not believe me. I can assure you that I know nothing. I even began laughing while I wrote this. Don't you see, I can laugh about these things called ultimate truth because I am free of the notion, know this quest to be absolutely ridiculous!

Myths on the other hand are a wild thing. If you're lucky and if you put your faith in dreams you will be able to drift in the invisible comfortably. This is not a particularly difficult place to travel, but it is hard to stay there. Everyone is capable of imagination and feelings. Many people feel that stories and dreams and myths are silly, childish, stupid components of a strange and undeveloped domain. People who think like this were raised to be serious and are addicted to spectating. Are addicted in some weird way to having others tell them stories on television, at the movies, in the entertainment periodicals. Not trusting what comes naturally is saddening.

Like I said, becoming lost in the invisible is available to anyone. You don't need a science to reveal the way you ought to feel, a religion to guide all your actions. Individualized feelings are all we have and believing this we are able to create. Our ideas of truth are what we feel to be real not facts. This is relatively obvious of course, but useful. I mean people smoke even though they know it increases their chance of dying. People say yes when they wish they'd said no. So we often live in an upside down world. To this I say great! Why do people act mean toward others? Because they have been confined in various ways and when set free, or notice people doing something different than what they think is fundamental, go crazy! It is only through cherishing everything, through loving everything that we can be free and in the "know." In my mind, only prayers, myths and nature can provide us with ways to try and attain these feelings.

How can anything I've said so far be reasonable? I've not talked about anything invisible, yet told you that the invisible is what we need. A tornado is pretty blatant. Sitting in a hallway playing the trombone is totally real. Having make-believe friends is mentally real. The catch is that only by living with a wide range of real things and ideas, only by feeling free and uncontrolled can people turn around and open up holes which then lead to their dreams, which then connect them with myths. Only by faith can people journey into the invisible and stay there comfortably.

Making the invisible come alive is not so impossible. Start with a simple crash course in philosophy. All around the world it turns out that people have been saying things like good is bad, black is white, life is death, the seen is not seen, love your enemy, the way is easy strive hard, nothing is something. Words are not real, Gods can not be defined. It turns out that it is normal to be confused. It turns out that you don't need to know the "truth" to be human. It turns out that things are not as they seem, yet completely what they are.

The only way to get into these ways of thinking is to delve where no words exist, to the invisible, to the everlasting. This is out of time, down where Alice is most likely still running around in Wonderland this very instant, where Christopher Robin is talking to Pooh Bear even as I write this very sentence now. Maybe it's where slips of the tongue lash out. That dream you know you had, but can't remember. Seeds that sprout inexplicably during the midst of a three year drought.

Lao-Tzu states, "The good runner leaves no tracks." Using this logic, the good thinker thinks no thoughts. At some point you have to give up on words and thought, blend into myths and stories, have to go out and be of the world, casting a fly line alongside the flow of eternal river, into the flow of life. Walk through the tall grove of Oak trees by your house. Step on to the podium you fear and speak. Ask the woman out on a date you've been thinking about for months, maybe years. I severely doubt that following facts can ever take you to that place between the sunset and the ground and if you really think about it, where else would you want to be.

I know that I don't believe facts and reason can take me to the color I am searching for. I don't believe that the everlasting shade of white light, vaguely tucked behind the wet and dripping, ethereal green glow of the disappearing wolverines will come back to me unless I think for myself, believe for myself, act for myself. This is a place of instinct and inner bliss. But only in surprise do you discover many of life's secrets. If I am really ready, then all of a sudden, someday, I will spot wolverines looking for me and only if in that split second I say *YES* without any hesitation, without any consciousness, will I really have changed.

Fortunately instinct is never far away. Intuition and the invisible live with us all the time. The phone rings and you know who it is. The wind smells like rain. Right before you get on your bike you check your tires and notice the sidewall is about to burst, you feel something hot behind your shoulder, turn around and there's a fox staring at you. It is a glorious day, the sun is golden across the just mown grass and you know this is the evening your grandfather will die. You dream of where you will find morel mushrooms. A deer walks right in front of you while hunting, but something inside you halts the aim and the trigger of your gun. You sit in the same spot long enough and suddenly a bird lands on you. All of these things are unexplainable, yet they are accurate moments, are see-through-solid moments, are moments when you really are standing between the sunset and the ground. They show you that the invisible is indeed working. You become a runner with no tracks. You become a trusting, confident, individual because you have faith in the unseen world which we all share.

8.

Like I said before, each morning I reach into the earth and pinch a small amount of clay from the ground. I roll this pinch of clay between my fingers, to form a bead, contemplate my breathing, notice birds flying, place the bead in my mouth, then swallow. This is my rosary dosage.

What's in a handful of earth? Everything. We all eat of the life of the soil. We were all born of dust. Crumbling between your fingers is the life and soul of creation, recreation, resurrection, hope, miracles and honesty. A tulip rests as a bear hibernating, feeding off the cold, arctic air that blows overhead, finally bursting forth with the brilliance of a portable sun in the spring. This is more than rhapsody, it is hope and fear overcome.

There's a fine line between innocence and sincerity, a fine line between being mad and being MAD! Some people are simply mad at the world for treating them so harshly. A MAD, neurotic individual, according to Joseph Campbell is one who can't figure out how to fit their dreams into the myths of a society. As a result they end up having to live, "out there" away from society and thus they either come to understand and overcome their fears, thereby becoming a "hero," or they sink into an isolation all full of terror and anxiety. I've never met anyone that isn't a little neurotic because everyone has a sympathetic, personal dream living in themselves somewhere, even if it's deeply repressed. It is sometimes hard to distinguish who's mad about not being able to follow their dreams and who is MAD from striving to follow their dreams.

Hopes and dreams and expectations are vital and tricky. How do you know if they are authentic. How can you be sure they haven't been devised by a scheming and constantly tricky, psychic marketing agency? Are they creative, do they seem uniquely yours, yet natural as a long lost friend? This is myth working.

Take Iowa for instance. If Iowa is okay, some say, then the whole nation is okay. We are the place that people think America is, was, ought to be. We are a fair and decent people. We are a land emitting soft cushions of creamy comfort, a region made up of ladies sitting in circles sewing quilts of virgin innocence. Where a man is a man and a woman is a woman. Where kids still get raised with family values and mud on their knees. We are simple folk, a naïve and literal people in love with our corn and hogs and our easy pace of comfortable life. We bake pies from apples that grow on the trees in our backyards. We cool these pies on our window sills and sometimes goofy, harmless kids like Randy and Earl sneak up and steal them. We all think this is worth laughter. Mr. Smith will say, "That lil' Earl, he sure is a funny one, that lil' ol' boy 'bout makes me crack a rib laughing."

Mrs. Smith, she says, "Remind me to give his mother a call tonight so that I make sure I get my pie pan back. I sure hope he and Randy liked the pie."

If you're not sitting on your front porch talking to friends on a crisp and delightful summer combed day in Iowa, then obviously you are weeding your garden. I mean we all wear overalls and have gardens. The corn is always higher than any bean stalk that ever went up to the dreamy heavens. And the cool autumn evenings, oh they are glorious and the dew in the morning, have you tasted it my friends, such concentrated elixir that you just gotta know redemption is nearby. Such flavor that it would cause your taste buds to explode in faultless rapture.

But doggone it, wouldn't you know it, this Iowa we think we know never has and never will exist. What place could? People have been tilling, trapping, cutting, polluting and destroying the place for generations. If you lived in Alaska could you imagine having only five percent of your cedar and spruce trees left. If you live along a river where salmon spawn can you imagine if literally only one or two salmon appeared. If you lived along the ocean could you imagine if there was only one wave a day? Did you know that only one tenth of one percent of the native plants that once existed in Iowa do now. Why do you think people ended up in California, Oregon, Washington and Alaska? Many of them tramped through Iowa, used it a few years and then moved on. The great sin of not paying attention was lived out and is still being lived out to its extreme in Iowa and the upper Midwest.

Paul Gruchow says Midwestern towns, "were planned as profit centers, not as communities." This is the real Iowa, a place to use and abuse, then leave. I don't know that you could still live in Iowa now if you didn't at least believe restoration was possible and worthwhile. Perhaps this explains why most of the people who live in Iowa wish they didn't. Why most people in the upper Midwest make fun of the place, talking about how they're going to move somewhere important one of these days real soon. Some people claim to like Iowa for instance, but they have great paying jobs and so live as though they were on the east coast anyway, all the while planning to use Iowa as a stepping stone in the near future.

As hard as it may seem, as unlikely as it would appear, the upper Midwest area, including Iowa is capable of providing real, enduring dreams and hope. People have, will and shall always be living brave and heroic lives amongst the rolling hills. This land is where I focus my prayers. This land is where my stories live since Iowa and the Midwest are my community and my home. There is no question that my dreams are coming alive here. Of course, I am a little mad, and a maybe even more MAD.

When I think of the abuse dished out to plants, soil and animals though I am ashamed. I have seen people swerve in the road to run over turtles, squirrels and rabbits; then honk their horn and peel out as though they had done something great. I've seen fly fisherman, who ought to respect clean water more than anyone, toss cigarette butts into creeks, leave their soda cans along the shore. People talk about the buckets and buckets of fish they've caught as though they deserve these fish, as if the fish are subspecies of life. People speak about the coyote they killed with glee, *"them dirty lazy bastards, all they do is steal anyway."* People walk around in their yards with poison, spraying individual dandelions, water their lawns during drought, never questioning why they need to purchase bottled water to drink. Writer Barry Lopez states in his book, The Rediscovery of North America, a sad and telling point which I wish were never true, a truth which has haunted those of us in the *New World.* It goes like this: Hours after Columbus claimed to have discovered this new place a process which has never really stopped began, "This incursion, this harmful road into the *New World* quickly became a ruthless, angry search for wealth." Thinking of this is disturbing especially if one understands all peoples, all things, all parts of this world to all be equal parts of a holy world.

Maybe I am too considerate for my own good though. When I am shooting down the highway in my automotive bullet and a raccoon appears in my headlights it is a wholly terrible thing to feel. To see it stare right at me, hunched so close to the ground and in such fear as I approach. I feel an unbelievable wash of embarrassment as I witness the raccoon issue a snarl and look at me with such fierceness and bravery. I will never experience this type of invasion, may never have to display such primal bravery. I hate to feel this unnatural inequity between myself and the animal. Whether I swerve just right, or stop in time, why should these acts become this, or any, animal's salvation. There is next to no justice, or compassion in this situation. I can only hope that in the Biblical sense all things really have been created equally and that the raccoon and all wild animals are capable of what we seldom seem to take the time to achieve, "to love your enemies and to pray for those persecuting you." (Matt. 5:44)

I can make no final judgement though. I am unable to offer some final dream. For one thing, Iowa is many things at once, like Walt Whitman says in his poem *Song of Myself*, "every atom good to me, as good belongs to you." Amongst the migration of people through the state, amongst the joyous fields of raspberries, along the little creeks, deep in the valleys, amongst the animals hit by cars, the spraying of herbicides, my psyche has been formed. When I say I don't want to leave this place I mean it physically, but also mentally. This land of Iowa, this glorious region of the upper Midwest has created me. It has a hold of me. The land is stretched out in even fields, dotted with rings of trees around farm steads. People poke fun of the painter Grant Wood as though he were making things up. I wonder, have these people seen Iowa in the spring? It turns out there are little green dots in rows curving over rolling hills. In many towns the tallest buildings still are the churches. There are hills that make you think of peace, there are cemeteries that sprout native grass and if you stand amongst these grasses and flowers you may easily spot a comet, or a shooting star flying through space. If you're lucky you may find a fresh peach pie waiting for you when you get home.

Very early in my life, on October mornings, I used to rest atop my neighbor's compost heap. I would lay on the pile of leaves and grass finding the heat beneath me soothing. I would sit there in silence before any of my friends woke up and look out at the chilly, frosted world around me. Listening to the little creek nearby and hearing the doves coo made me feel the gift of dreams and satisfaction. The world seemed to fill me up with joy. This type of feeling is one of my measures for satisfaction and rarely have I felt so content, but from time to time, while playing, running, walking, loving, being with my child, my wife, my family, friends, usually outdoors somewhere, I still get this joyful feeling of full satisfaction with life and mystery and love.

Let's say I do agree with 99% of the population, maybe this land of Iowa with its creeks and sunsets does offer nothing spectacular. But even if 99% of the people are correct 99% of the time this still leaves open the hint of mirages and bliss 1% of the time. There is still the chance of becoming enveloped in that place I mentioned. Of one day stepping out of the shadow of a tree right into that dream world, smack dab between sunset and the ground. I can only live thinking that I may be able to walk off with the wolverines to that place we all wonder about deep in our hearts where joy and dreams come true.

It is during still moments by ourselves when we ask questions like, *What am I going to do with my life? Who am I? What do I mean? What mistakes have I made? Am I really happy?* Or sometimes, instead of asking questions we simply raise our hands and thank God for the way things are! In some ways then, if Iowa is okay then everything is okay. And guess what, it turns out Iowa is okay. In moments of sunrise and sunset, while out on a lone country road on a bike Iowa does come alive and every atom that is good to me is good for you.

Witness: when the sun goes down some nights I see pheasants bolting out of the grass, spot wild turkeys eeking out along the edge of corn fields, spot shadows spilling into the dark woods. These are the real things I believe in and what spur my needs to create and cherish the world. This could be called innocence, or being naïve. So be it. As you now know I have no problems with these ways of being alive.

Simplifying confusion helps though. What is really simple and normal? Not the double garage, with a house payment and car loan, a square green lawn with a narrowly defined college fund for the kids. Most of these things are tied up in the complexities of capitalism and employee dependency, in the deadening and deafening world of group-think, of majority rules kind of stuff. Simple and more real is perhaps canning tomatoes. Concocting a hinge out of scrap metal instead of hopping in the car and driving to the hardware store to buy one. Simple is thanking the world for blue herons, brown trout, juicy plums, for good poetry, fine writing, wonderful art and singing. Thanking rain drops and mushrooms when they appear. Simple is really just thinking for yourself and feeling independent and competent, free and in tune with the world. Gary Snyder has a beautiful description of a simple moment, a moment we can all understand in his essay, *The Etiquette of Freedom*. A "calm and clarity attend us in the moment we are wiping grease off our hands between tasks and glancing up at the passing clouds."

Being simple is living amongst all the elements of the world and paying our regards, accepting what IS as beautiful. It is not thinking what next, how much money I don't have, why such and such has such when they only do such and such and by God such and such better not do that one thing again because that's totally a bunch of such and such … . New adventures in life, new jobs, new goals, new hopes really can be enjoyed and trusted.

Here's a contradiction though, a twist. It turns out that there is a secret in life. And it goes like this: mystic expectations are real. If you look hard enough there are trout in the streams, there are clearings in the trees where songbirds are dancing and making music, there is earth still so rich and thick and deep and loamy it is way beyond belief. For instance, one simply can't imagine the depth and the beauty that five acres of Iowa topsoil can produce, it is the Earth Mother at full glory. The depth of prairie grass roots is unimaginable. The drift of clouds blow the numeric restrictions of calculus clean away. To think that mystics are glorified estimators, or lucky guessers is nonsense. Rumi writes, "Mystics will feel very happy, as a meadow feels when it hears thunder."

If you treat the world with prayer and honesty and respect you do yourself a favor and the world stays in balance and you are able to stand by your words and heart. Treating the world as an experiment is fine in theory, but theory is not a breathing, eating, drinking, spontaneous entity. Poetry and music and imagination are life at its fullest. Not because they reveal the truth, but because they are independent and creative. They are individualized sacraments to being alive in what is an unexplainable and unique universe.

It is no small comment that if asparagus and mushrooms continue to return each year then reality is complete. If you take them for granted, then you've lost the thread of life, for these returns are the circles and spirals of your breath, your heart, your family, your hopes, rituals and dreams. None of these ideas may hold water, they are just my beliefs. They are as much a new testament, as an old. If you'd prefer you can call them reading the wild testament.

In this vain, the bread and the blood are all abounding. The creation of spirits is, in a round about way, like concocting elixir. Many Christians engage in drinking the blood of Christ which is valid and something I totally respect and admire. I do so too. I journey with the wine and the earth when I make wine and when I sip it I feel engaged in journey.

I would recommend that we all create our own local spirits, or earth blood. Wander the land and pick blackberries. Engage in the slow making of the world and engage with the symbolisms you cherish. Find the fruit, take the hours and days needed to gather and pick. Shed your own blood on the cleated thorns of the blackberry, then do the cleaning, weighing, squashing, fermenting, corking. Experience and become part of the wine as it settles and mellows and takes on the flavor of the kiss of the Buddha. This is the celebration and wonder of being alive is it not!

The wafer, the body? Why not make it a regional delicacy that arises in cycles throughout the year. In

Iowa for instance, why not the morel mushroom, which normally appears for the first time around Easter. Such glory and flavor, such a radiant offering from the earth and something which we can savor and honor and mark our passage through life with. How well we might feel if we tended what we believed to be vital to our well being. To my mind you go on both an inward and an outward journey following these ideas.

Maybe I am a heretic, or iconoclastic or something worse, but I don't think so. Blood is a life force. The earth runs from water, producing grains, deer, tomatoes, grapes, oaks, mushrooms, coyote, raven, eggplant, caves. Cherish the earth by drinking of all its bloods, acknowledging and recognizing the body and spirit of where you live.

Finale

I don't want to continue the mistakes of others, not being taught reverence for miracles, have to learn the importance of cycles during the year, have to understand that baking bread is an holy act, have to figure out how to learn respect for prayer and the need to give thanks to the Holy spirit alive throughout the world. I refuse to believe what my teachers instilled in me: to think there was no reason to care about the place I grew up, or that everyone ought to learn and act and behave the same. I refuse to believe that there is only one way to live and one proper moral path to follow. Refuse to believe that I was inadequate.

I was tempted, very tempted to take the first road out of town and never come back to Iowa and the Midwest in my life, but I didn't. I harbored some unexplainable apprehension about leaving the place where I had come to life in. I was weary of abandoning the spots that I had engaged with so intimately and which have provided me with most of what I know. Some doors open with every decision we make, some close with each decision we make. Some things I will never understand fully: never leaving your hometown for instance. It is too easy to say not leaving is naive. The people I know who have never left often seem quite content to me. Many of us will never even touch the real meaning of marriage, or of place. There is never an end, or simple path to claiming knowledge. We can only pretend to know anything and we would all do well to respect that. It makes no sense, but knowing the world through confusion is what really makes sense.

This is partly how I've come to these conclusions: I believed in seeing tadpoles turned to frogs. Watched eggs hatch into birds. Craved the skills of building, planning, sawing, hammering. These skills have empowered me in my life. I have never known what's going on in the world, have never watched, listenined, or much cared about the news. I was not exposed to prayer and worship as I child. I was expected to live at the elementary moral level of a six year old, in that spot where there is no clear understanding of respect and where all things were somehow simply defined as good, or bad. That good would allow you to continue as you were and that bad would somehow result in the worst of conditions, not only while alive but on into an afterlife of fire and damnation. Without being exposed to contemplation, or thoughtful spirituality I became stunted as a person, remaining stoic, confused, afraid and morally bound by my childish stereotypes for many years. So immature as to be scared to think for myself. Unable to venture into chance.

Fortunately my life has mostly been lived outdoors and the natural world became my realm of resurrection and worship. I discovered that if you didn't understand mud well enough your foot would sink to your knee and you'd lose your shoe and leave a big sucking, deep hole in the earth. Without knowing it the ever changing world of nature initiated me into prayers with plant life, showed me the concept of the eternal through seasons and equinoxes. I discovered the value of both feeling blessed by, and of giving blessings and offerings to the land. I felt the need to give eulogies on solstices for the living animals, the top soil and to the God, or Spirit which must be existent for all of this to be.

I remember when I was a little kid we made a bird feeder for an owl down in the woods. One night we offered it food and during the evening, while watching from behind a large log, the owl thanked us with his arrival. There is no shame in learning to worship on your own, sometimes with friends, out in the wilds. Whether you learn in a church, or behind a fallen tree, either one will lead you to experience an inner rapture. Each will let you find a richness to life which convinces that the earth and human emotions, cycles and compassion will not wear out, or let you down.

If a loved one dies unexpectedly during the winter know that in the spring life will reappear and offer you hope and that the spirit of birth always comes as a result of death, they are one and the same and in fact one is offered and sacrificed for the other to occur. Spring is always happening, falls are going on all the time. This is obvious and often said, but still it isn't always clear and there seems to be a need and a reassurance in hearing these sorts of things said out loud and often.

The small Buddhist story *Kisagotami* points this out. When Kisagotami's young child dies unexpectedly she agonizes alone, as anyone would, until she is told by a holy man to find out if she is truly alone in this suffering. Lo and behold she finds that everyone around her lives with death, has suffered from tragedy, "All living beings resemble the flame of lamps, one moment lighted, the next extinguished." This brings her a level of solace.

To this I say, move lightly then, as invisibly as possible. Discover hidden secrets in the forms of mushrooms, and bats. Hear the sound of a kingfisher, a loon, imitate the glimmers of fire flies in your heart and make your breath hiss from time to time as though standing next to a hornets nest. I make prayers to this land where I live because this place holds me stable and proud and gives me hope. Roots me to all of life and creativity and futures beyond eternity. I believe in miracles because miracles find us and return us to ourselves, take us to that place between the sunset and the ground, allow the wolverines to appear just like that. It takes much effort, but why not do as the Taoist koan states, "The way is easy, strive hard." Strive to experience each moment completely anew. Live with easy breath, think of terribly wonderful things. For me anyway this is the way I have come to believe that I am no more than a seed and that my words and life and thoughts and dreams sprout and grow from the ground!

like this!

The mighty mississippi river during a flood, all bloodshot and grueling with mounds of majestic mudsnot foam. The wind has cracked the umbilical cord of the trees and the earth is all full and bending. The very atoms I am breathing splinter in my throat. A full black lustered fire taunts me to reach up and grab the wind. I wonder, is almighty Brahma rocking back and forth, has the dream spirit Vishnu shaken his head? Is he dreaming of the ever taunting great white whale, that creature haunting Captain Ahab, I wonder if even at this moment has that fleshy ghost Moby Dick surfaced jaw agape?

And then I am hoping, looking at the earth spinning in it's slow and wonderful way, the sun playing it's setting role. I am overlooking the Iowa river, the spring rains falling, my feet merging with the ground, tapping into the earth and if I am lucky and ready maybe, finally, perhaps by chance the Wolverines will appear to me again, all elemental bright, full of the creation of the world, of light and spirit, water and fire, earth and air. This time I would join them. O to be a wolverine burrowing in the dirt, fulfilled with the treasures of the natural world. This would be integration, living free and real without a trail. So I chant of the Krishna, sing in honor of the Lord's Holy Trinity, think of the Buddha shedding karma, envision water splitting granite. Watch the flight of a blue heron; wishing always for the words of the Wolverine, for that coloring so subtle when the sunset squeaks and splashes so lightly over everything, just barely into the ground and is able to tickle the roots of the deepest, oldest trees.

and then
this is how my days end.
There is a glow
coming from my sternum
where the bead
I swallowed this morning
has been kilned

by the very
real degrees of the earth
bloomed
eternal
invisible
mystery
all around
inside
and which now ends
as the moon rises
presenting itself
as yet another
bead
of the
never
fully
ever
known

•

Printer's device by
Andy Driscoll

Established in 1993, the Ice Cube Press is a small, independent press dedicated to publishing writing on nature, the environment and regionalism.

Ice Cube Press
205 North Front Street
North Liberty, Iowa 52317-9302
icecube@inav.net
www.icecubepress.com

out